CAMPAIGN 425

# KOKODA 1942–43

Japanese Defeat in Papua

**PETER WILLIAMS**  ILLUSTRATED BY JOHNNY SHUMATE

OSPREY PUBLISHING
Bloomsbury Publishing Plc
Kemp House, Chawley Park, Cumnor Hill, Oxford OX2 9PH, UK
Bloomsbury Publishing Ireland Limited,
29 Earlsfort Terrace, Dublin 2, D02 AY28, Ireland
Bloomsbury Publishing Inc.
1359 Broadway, 12th Floor, New York, NY 10018, USA
E-mail: info@ospreypublishing.com
www.ospreypublishing.com

OSPREY is a trademark of Osprey Publishing Ltd

First published in Great Britain in 2026

© Osprey Publishing Ltd, 2026

All rights reserved. No part of this publication may be: i) reproduced or transmitted in any form, electronic or mechanical, including photocopying, recording or by means of any information storage or retrieval system without prior permission in writing from the publishers; or ii) used or reproduced in any way for the training, development or operation of artificial intelligence (AI) technologies, including generative AI technologies. The rights holders expressly reserve this publication from the text and data mining exception as per Article 4(3) of the Digital Single Market Directive (EU) 2019/790

A catalogue record for this book is available from the British Library.

ISBN: PB 9781472869821; eBook 9781472869814; ePDF 9781472869807;
XML 9781472869838

26 27 28 29 30   10 9 8 7 6 5 4 3 2 1

Maps by Bounford.com
3D BEVs by Paul Kime
Index by Alan Rutter
Typeset by Lumina Datamatics Ltd
Printed by Repro India Ltd

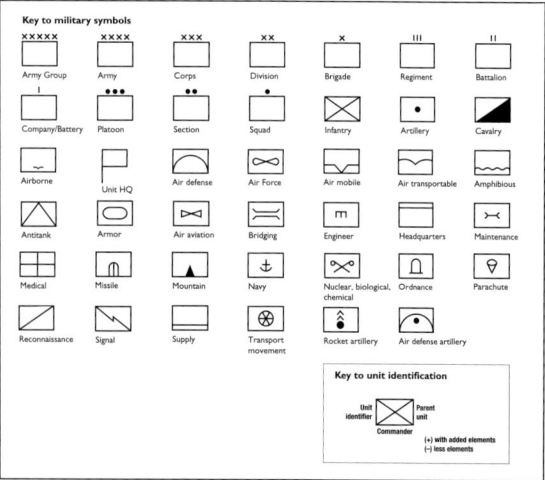

## Author's note

Japanese names appear with the family name first. Japanese units are in italics. All other units are American, Australian or Papuan, apart from ship names, which also appear in italics. The Allied Air Force (AAF) was divided into two: the 5th US Army Air Force (which included Australian squadrons) and RAAF Command. Almost all operations in Papua were conducted by the 5th US Army Air Force, which is the term used here.

The Kokoda Trail is also known as the Kokoda Track, especially in Australia. I have used Trail throughout.

## Acknowledgements

The author would like to thank Phillip Bradley, Michael Claringbould, David Jenkins and David Howell for their assistance with this book.

## Dedication

For Joseph Hermann Thureau, TX8226, 2/12th Australian Infantry Battalion. Joe told me stories of the Papuan Campaign when I was a boy in Tasmania.

## Editor's note

For ease of comparison please refer to the following conversion table:
1 mile = 1.6 kilometres
1 yard = 0.9 metres
1 pound = 0.45 kilograms

## Glossary

| | |
|---|---|
| AAF | Allied Air Force |
| AIF | Australian Imperial Force |
| ANGAU | Australian New Guinea Administrative Unit |
| CMF | Citizen Military Forces |
| ER | Engineer Regiment |
| IER | Independent Engineer Regiment |
| IHQ | Imperial Headquarters (Tokyo) |
| IJA | Imperial Japanese Army |
| IJN | Imperial Japanese Navy |
| MFHQ | Maroubra Force Headquarters |
| NGF | New Guinea Force |
| NP | Naval Pioneers |
| NSHQ | *Nankai Shitai* Headquarters |
| PIB | Papuan Infantry Battalion |
| RAAF | Royal Australian Air Force |
| RAN | Royal Australian Navy |
| RCT | Regimental Combat Team |
| RGC | Regimental Gun Company |
| RHQ | Regimental Headquarters |
| RPC | Royal Papuan Constabulary |
| SNLF | Special Naval Landing Force |
| SWPA | South West Pacific Area |
| USAAF | United States Army Air Force |
| USN | United States Navy |

Osprey Publishing supports the Woodland Trust, the UK's leading woodland conservation charity.

To find out more about our authors and books visit www.ospreypublishing.com. Here you will find extracts, author interviews, details of forthcoming events and the option to sign up for our newsletter.

For product safety related questions contact productsafety@bloomsbury.com

**Front cover main illustration:** Brigade Hill, 8 September 1942. (Johnny Shumate)
**Title page photograph:** 32nd Division advancing on Buna, 15 November 1942. (Afro American Newspapers/Gado/Getty Images)

# CONTENTS

## ORIGINS OF THE CAMPAIGN 5
Japanese ■ Allied

## CHRONOLOGY 8

## OPPOSING COMMANDERS 10
Japanese ■ Allied

## OPPOSING FORCES 14
Japanese ■ Allied ■ Orders of battle

## OPPOSING PLANS 20
Japanese ■ Allied

## THE CAMPAIGN 23
The Japanese advance on the Kokoda Trail ■ Guadalcanal ■ Milne Bay ■ The Japanese retreat ■ Preparations for an Allied thrust ■ The battle of Buna–Gona ■ Australian front – the first two weeks ■ American front – the first two weeks ■ The *coup de main* fails ■ Command ■ Warren front in December ■ Urbana front in December ■ December on the Australian front ■ Supply ■ January on the American front ■ January on the Australian front ■ Breakout ■ Summing up

## AFTERMATH 90

## THE BATTLEFIELDS TODAY 92
Port Moresby ■ Kokoda Trail ■ Milne Bay ■ Buna–Gona

## FURTHER READING 94

## INDEX 95

# Japanese operations in the Solomon Sea, January–August 1942

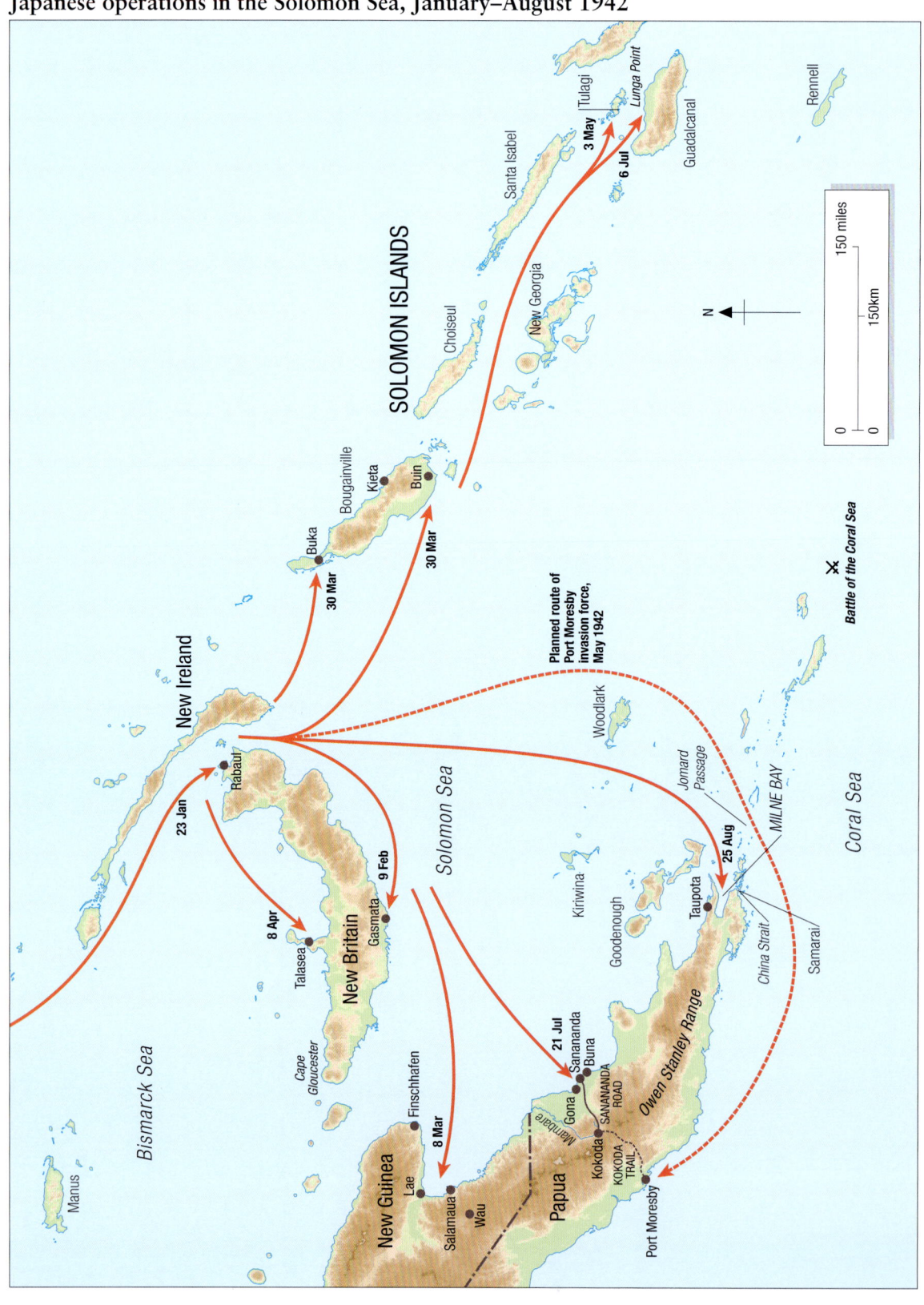

# ORIGINS OF THE CAMPAIGN

## JAPANESE

By July 1942, having captured the oil of the Dutch East Indies, Japan had achieved its main war aim. Japanese strategy in the Pacific was now to build a defensive barrier to prepare for the expected Allied counter-attack, which was predicted to come from Australia within six months, making the 'southern seas' the key theatre in 1942 from the Japanese perspective. A United States Navy (USN) offensive from the west coast of the US via Hawaii was, rightly, believed to be more than a year away. No thought was

*144th Regiment*, part of the *Nankai Shitai*, enters Rabaul, 23 January 1942. (Author's Collection)

given to a threat to the Solomon Islands, where the Imperial Japanese Navy (IJN) was building an airfield at Guadalcanal to enable air attacks on the US to Australia shipping route.

To fend off the Allied counter-attack, a new major fleet and air base was required. Rabaul, in New Britain, the finest harbour in the region, was selected. However, it was most undesirable that Rabaul was within range of the four Allied airfields at Port Moresby. Vice Admiral Inoue Shigeyoshi, commander *4th Fleet*, expressed the view that Rabaul was simply not a viable base if the fleet at anchor could be regularly bombed. From February to July 1942, Australian and American aircraft, based at or staging through Port Moresby, had made 20 raids, albeit small ones, on Rabaul, 500 miles away.

A second consideration was that Imperial Headquarters (IHQ) saw Australia as the only country in Allied hands in the western Pacific with the industry, agriculture, developed ports, airfields, population and transport to support a counter-attack. With Australia's war-making capacities concentrated in the east, bounded by Brisbane, Adelaide, Melbourne and Sydney – the rest of the vast continent had poor communications and infrastructure – any offensive would originate from that coast directed at Rabaul via the two Australian Territories of Papua and New Guinea. It followed that the Allies would need the only useful port with airfields on the south coast of Papua, Port Moresby. If the Japanese held Port Moresby, this route would be closed.

IHQ had decided in March that it was beyond their means to conquer Australia. As a measure of their shift to a defensive stance in the Pacific, in June they abandoned plans to capture New Caledonia, Samoa, Fiji and Espiritu Santo. However, Australia's use as the Allied springboard for a counteroffensive, and the fact that Port Moresby was within bombing range of Rabaul, prompted aggressive action within the otherwise defensive Japanese posture.

The first attempt to capture Port Moresby failed at the battle of the Coral Sea. Following the loss of four carriers at Midway, the IJN was no longer willing to risk carriers in the confined waters of the Solomon or Coral Seas. There was, however, another option. There was a viable approach from the north coast of Papua, near Buna, where a route led to Kokoda, then over the Owen Stanley Range to the back door of Port Moresby. In addition, the Rabaul–Buna sea route was 200 miles north of that to Port Moresby via the Jomard Passage or China Strait into the Coral Sea. Japanese aircraft at Lae, Gasmata and Rabaul could cover the transports along this northern route without the need for carriers. Allied air power would also be less effective with the additional distance. On 14 June, Hyakutake Harukichi, *17th Army* commander in Rabaul, was told to begin the Papua operation using the Buna option.

# ALLIED

In early 1942, Australians feared an invasion. With the fall of Singapore, Timor, Ambon and Rabaul (January–February 1942), 19,000 Australian soldiers, sailors and airmen went into Japanese captivity and the Japanese were now within 300 miles of Australia. Two divisions of the Australian

Imperial Force (AIF), their best troops, were recalled from the Middle East. Six militia infantry divisions, an armoured and two mechanized divisions were undergoing hasty training in Australia, while the US sent the two-division 1st Corps.

Australia adopted a strategy of continental defence, with one exception; Port Moresby on the south coast of Papua, south of the Owen Stanley Range and 180 miles north-east of the closest part of Australia, would be held. In addition, a small guerrilla force, maintained from Port Moresby, watched the new Japanese bases at Lae and Salamaua in the Territory of New Guinea, 200 miles north of Port Moresby and where the Japanese landed on 8 March. Understanding as well as the Japanese that Port Moresby was the gateway to the east coast of Australia, and an essential asset in any future Allied counteroffensive, the Australians strengthened their garrison there.

General Douglas MacArthur, ordered to leave the Philippines three weeks before it fell, arrived in Australia on 17 March 1942. On 18 April he was designated Commander South West Pacific Area, headquartered in Melbourne. MacArthur maintained the Australian strategy, calling it 'a defence of the mainland from the Owen Stanley Range'.

As the threat of the invasion of Australia eased with the battles of the Coral Sea and Midway, the Joint Chiefs of Staff in Washington DC looked to use 1st US Corps, together with Australian troops, for an offensive. On 1 July, MacArthur was told his long-term objective was to recapture Rabaul. The first step was to retake Salamaua and Lae. Port Moresby would be the forward base while Milne Bay, on the eastern tip of Papua, would provide a useful harbour and airfields. One more thing was needed, an air base on the north side of the Owen Stanley Range. The weather in the range was extremely disruptive to air operations: an airfield on the north coast was essential to protect shipping, which had to pass that way from Milne Bay to attack Lae. The area around Buna looked promising on an otherwise swampy coastline, and on 11 July 1942, US engineers flew to Buna to see for themselves. They found Dobodura, 15 miles south of Buna, a suitable site which met their requirement for several all-weather strips that could be turned into a large airfield complex. Plans were made to garrison Buna strongly and forward the engineers and equipment needed for construction. The Japanese and the Allies were on a collision course, but the Japanese got to Buna first, nine days after the engineers left there to report back to Port Moresby.

Poster issued by the Australian Federal Government in early 1942. The Queensland State Government considered it too alarmist and refused to allow it to appear in that state. (IanDagnall Computing/Alamy Stock Photo)

# CHRONOLOGY

**1942**

| | |
|---|---|
| 23 January | Japanese land in Rabaul |
| 3 February | First Allied air raid on Rabaul and first Japanese air raid on Port Moresby |
| 8 March | Japanese land on mainland New Guinea at Lae and Salamaua |
| 18 April | MacArthur appointed Commander-in-Chief South West Pacific Area |
| 4–8 May | Battle of the Coral Sea |
| 4–7 June | Battle of Midway |
| 14 June | Japanese decide to attack Port Moresby along the Kokoda Trail (Track) |
| 1 July | Joint Chiefs of Staff order MacArthur to make limited offensive directed at Rabaul |
| 11–12 July | Dobodura, near Buna, identified by US engineers as suitable for airfields for the Rabaul offensive |
| 21 July | Advanced force of the *Nankai Shitai* (South Seas Force) lands at Basabua, near Buna |
| 23 July | First engagement of the campaign. The Papuan Infantry Battalion ambushes the Japanese at Awala on the Sanananda road |
| 29 July | First Kokoda – Japanese capture Kokoda |
| 7 August | US Marines land at Guadalcanal and Tulagi |
| 8–10 August | Second Kokoda – Australians briefly recapture Kokoda |
| 12–14 August | Deniki – Australian defeat |
| 19–21 August | Main body of *Nankai Shitai* arrives in Papua |
| 25 August | Japanese *Special Naval Landing Force* lands at Milne Bay |
| 26–31 August | Battle of Isurava – Japanese capture Isurava |
| 1–5 September | First Eora – Australian rearguard action |
| 5–6 September | Japanese *Special Naval Landing Force* evacuate Milne Bay |
| 6–9 September | Efogi/Brigade Hill – Australian defeat |
| 14–16 September | Ioribaiwa Ridge – Australian defeat |

| | |
|---|---|
| 23 September | General Blamey arrives at Port Moresby to take command of New Guinea Force |
| 24 September | Japanese retreat on Kokoda Trail begins |
| 28 September | Australian advance on the Kokoda Trail begins |
| 5 October | First Allied troops airlifted to north coast of Papua |
| 11–28 October | Second Eora–Templeton's – Australian victory |
| 2 November | Kokoda recaptured |
| 4–11 November | Oivi–Gorari – Australian victory. Japanese driven back to Buna |
| 16 November | MacArthur arrives in Port Moresby and battle of Buna–Gona begins |
| 26 November | Japanese *8th Area Army* takes over operations in Papua and Guadalcanal. *17th Army* assumes responsibility for Guadalcanal, *18th Army* for Papua and New Guinea |
| 29 November | Lieutenant General Herring arrives to take command at Buna |
| 30 November | Lieutenant General Eichelberger meets MacArthur in Port Moresby |
| 30 November | Huggins roadblock established |
| 2 December | Major General Harding relieved at Buna. Replaced by Eichelberger |
| 9 December | Gona captured |
| 14 December | Buna village captured |
| 18 December | First attack with tank support. Cape Endiadere captured |
| 26 December | The Triangle evacuated by the Japanese |

## 1943

| | |
|---|---|
| 1–2 January | Giropa Point captured |
| 2 January | Buna Government Station captured |
| 14 January | Japanese ordered to evacuate Papua |
| 16 January | Japanese evacuate position at junction of Sanananda road and Cape Killerton track |
| 20 January | Japanese breakout begins |
| 22 January | All organized Japanese resistance ceases. Papuan Campaign ends |

# OPPOSING COMMANDERS

## JAPANESE

**Lieutenant General Hyakutake Harukichi (1888–1947)** was a graduate of the Imperial Japanese Army Academy. Marked out for early promotion, he rose to divisional command in China in the late 1930s. In May 1942, he was sent to Rabaul to command *17th Army*. Responsible at first for both the Solomons and Papua, he had under him the *Nankai Shitai* (*South Seas Force*), which invaded Papua. Hyakutake was among those who argued, in August 1942, that the American attack on Guadalcanal was the more important operation and the advance in Papua should be put on hold while the Guadalcanal problem was solved. A competent general, and an expert codebreaker, he greatly increased the cryptography cell in Rabaul in 1942. He survived the war.

Lieutenant General Hyakutake Harukichi. (Author's Collection)

**Major General Horii Tomitaro (1890–1942)** served in China, then was given command of the *Nankai Shitai* in 1941. He led the force in the captures of Guam (where he was briefly governor), Rabaul, Lae and Salamaua, and then Papua. His well-planned advance along the Kokoda Trail was derailed by the decision that the advance on Port Moresby must halt to send reinforcements to Guadalcanal instead of Papua. Horii's great mistake in the campaign was the failure of his plan to annihilate the Australians at Isurava. Horii drowned attempting to escape after the Japanese defeat at Oivi–Gorari.

**Colonel Kusunose Masao (1899–1946)** was the most successful Japanese commander of the campaign. Kusunose, commander of *144th Regiment*, led a fast pursuit of the Australians on the Kokoda Trail. He won two fine victories at Efogi/Brigade Hill and Ioribaiwa. Ill with malaria, Kusunose commanded the second battle from a litter as he was carried about the battlefield. Failing to recover, he was evacuated in late October 1942, replaced by one of his battalion commanders, Colonel Tsukamoto Hatsuo. Surviving the war, Kusunose was called to a war crimes tribunal in Tokyo for murders committed by his troops in New Britain, in particular the Tol Plantation massacre. Ignoring the summons, he fled to the foot of Mount Fuji and starved himself to death.

**LEFT**
Major General Horii Tomitaro. (Public domain via Wikimedia Commons)

**RIGHT**
Colonel Kusunose Masao. (Author's Collection)

Lieutenant General Yamagata Tsuyuo (1890–1945) was a colonel in 1937, when he saw action in China. Promoted to command of *21st Mixed Brigade* in 1941, his brigade was sent to reinforce the Buna garrison. He was placed in command of all Japanese forces at Buna–Gona on 2 December 1942. On receiving orders to evacuate Papua, Yamagata took it upon himself to advance the timetable. He organized the evacuation of the wounded and planned a breakout of the garrison. He was killed in action in Pampanga Province, Philippines, in April 1945.

# ALLIED

### Americans

**General Douglas MacArthur (1880–1964)** commanded the South West Pacific Area (SWPA), within which was Papua. He had seen action at Vera Cruz, and on the Western Front during World War I. Resigning from the US Army, he became military advisor to the Government of the Philippines. He was recalled to active duty in the US Army in July 1941 and was in command during the Japanese invasion of the Philippines in December. In March 1942, MacArthur was ordered to Australia by President Roosevelt. There, he was placed in command of the SWPA.

MacArthur maintained good relations with the Australian Prime Minister John Curtin, but many in his government felt Curtin sacrificed too much sovereignty by allowing an American general to make decisions on Australia's future at a time when Australians believed they faced invasion. During the Papuan Campaign, MacArthur and the Australian generals had a sometimes turbulent relationship; the majority of the land forces MacArthur commanded were Australians, but their fate was decided by Americans:

Generals Douglas MacArthur, Thomas Blamey and Arthur Allen (left to right). Allen is receiving advice from MacArthur before he departs for the Kokoda Trail to take command of 7th Division's advance in September 1942. (Author's Collection)

**LEFT**
Lieutenant General Robert Eichelberger. (Public domain via Wikimedia Commons)

**RIGHT**
Major General Edwin Harding. (Public domain via Wikimedia Commons)

the ten senior positions in MacArthur's General Headquarters in Melbourne were all held by his countrymen.

**Lieutenant General Robert Eichelberger (1886–1961)** had pre-World War II service in Panama, Mexico and Siberia, during the Russian Civil War. He arrived in Australia in August 1942 to take command of 1st Corps. Eichelberger's fear that his corps was undertrained and would not meet the Japanese on equal terms was justified when 32nd Division suffered serious reverses in its first month at Buna. MacArthur sent Eichelberger to Buna to relieve Harding, the division's commander. Eichelberger remained at Buna commanding the 32nd and a regiment of 41st Division. Towards the end of the battle, he took over from Herring all forces in the Buna area, including the Australian 7th Division.

**Major General Edwin Harding (1886–1970)** graduated from the United States Military Academy in the same class as Jacob Devers, George Patton and Robert Eichelberger. He served in the Philippines and on the Mexican border, rose to command 27th Infantry Regiment and became a brigadier general in 1941. On 9 February 1942, Harding was given command of 32nd Division. He trained the division in Australia then led it in combat at Buna–Gona for two weeks, before being replaced by Eichelberger. Opinion is divided on whether Harding's sacking was justified.

## *Australians*

**General Thomas Blamey (1884–1951)** was commander of Allied Land Forces in SWPA 1942–45. Staff college trained, Blamey, like all Australian generals in this campaign, had over three years active service in World War I. His career between the wars as Police Commissioner for the state of Victoria was marred by scandal when his police badge was found in a brothel.

In the Middle East in World War II, he commanded a division, a corps and then the AIF. Returning to Australia, he commanded all SWPA land forces. Blamey was sent by MacArthur to Papua when it appeared Port Moresby was about to fall. This precipitated a command crisis as his arrival usurped the position of New Guinea Force (NGF) commander, Sydney Rowell, who was fired. The only Australian to reach the rank of field marshal, Blamey

**LEFT**
Lieutenant General Edmund Herring. (History and Art Collection/Alamy Stock Photo)

**RIGHT**
Major General George Vasey. (Australian War Memorial 052620)

was a more than competent commander who maintained good relations with MacArthur.

**Lieutenant General Edmund Herring (1892–1982)** commanded all land forces in Papua. An artilleryman, he served four years in World War I, commanded the guns during the capture of Bardia and Tobruk in 1941 and later served in Greece. When Blamey dismissed Major General Rowell as Commander, New Guinea Force in September 1942, Herring replaced him. In November, Herring moved from Port Moresby to Buna, taking over all Allied forces there.

Herring believed his principal task during the battle of Buna–Gona was to ensure a good working relationship between the Australians and the Americans. He thought MacArthur an excellent general and was a close friend of Blamey.

**Major General George Vasey (1895–1945)** served on the Western Front from 1916 to 1918, in both combat and staff commands. In World War II, he commanded a brigade in North Africa, Greece and Crete. Returning to Australia he became, at 46, the youngest general in the army. Vasey replaced Major General Arthur Allen as Commander, 7th Division in October 1942, leading the division to victories at Oivi–Gorari and Buna–Gona. A professional soldier admired by his troops, Vasey died in a plane crash in 1945.

# OPPOSING FORCES

## JAPANESE

The Japanese combat units that invaded Papua in July 1942, the *Nankai Shitai*, were well-trained experienced veterans. Recent victories in Malaya, Guam and Rabaul had boosted their morale. They were superior in fighting power to any equal number of Australians or Americans they faced, until the hazards of climate, disease and malnutrition wore them down to defeat.

### *Imperial Japanese Army (IJA) infantry and artillery*
The two infantry regiments of the *Nankai Shitai*, with three battalions each, the *144th* and *41st Regiments*, were old China campaigners. The *144th* was recruited from the steep mountains of Shikoku. As veterans told this author, the rugged Owen Stanley Range in Papua held no terrors for them. The *41st*, which the *144th* considered to be soft city boys, was raised in Hiroshima but proved to be as good as the *144th*. Later arrivals from *170th* and *229th Regiments* were also high-quality infantry.

The Japanese put a huge effort into transporting disassembled artillery to remote battlefields, giving them an advantage their opponents did not have on the Kokoda Trail. Sixteen field artillery pieces came to Papua with the *Nankai Shitai*. Thirteen were lost in early November after the Japanese defeat at Oivi–Gorari. Another mountain gun battalion with 12 pieces landed in time for Buna–Gona and three guns were with the *Special Naval Landing Force (SNLF)* at Milne Bay. The guns were of three main types: 75mm mountain gun, 70mm infantry support and 37mm anti-tank guns, which could also fire high explosive.

Type 41 75mm gun, weight 1,200lb. In rough country, it could be taken apart to be carried by 18 men. Almost 1,000 of the 3,500 Japanese who entered the Owen Stanley Range carried disassembled artillery or ammunition for it in addition to their normal load. (Author's Collection)

### *IJN Special Naval Landing Force*
Often mistakenly thought to be marines, the *SNLF* were sailors with basic infantry training. Their primary task was to guard navy bases. The United States War

Department handbook on Japanese forces accurately described the *SNLF* as having 'a surprising lack of ability in infantry combat'. None fought in the Kokoda phase of the campaign. In the one operation in Papua they attempted alone, Milne Bay, the *SNLF* performed poorly. About 3,000 fought in Papua.

## Logistical support

The IJA was not well supplied by Western standards. The Japanese fought their campaigns on rice, tinned fish, soy paste and little else. Western troops expected more in their ration: cigarettes, chocolate, jam, biscuits, chewing gum and cheese spread. The Japanese were similarly frugal in forwarding munitions and fuel and eliminated weight in packaging. This sparse supply system worked well for them in China. Its advantage was, on average, 1,000 Japanese could fight on four tons of supplies of all kinds each day. Western armies in the Pacific aimed to send forward 22 tons per day per 1,000 men, but found in Papua only 12 tons was possible in the best circumstances. Until heavy rain in September 1942 wrecked the Japanese supply line from Buna to the Kokoda Trail, the *Nankai Shitai* was adequately supplied. Similarly, until the sea lane between Rabaul and Buna was made unsafe by Allied airpower, the Japanese in the Buna phase of the campaign were, with exceptions, sufficiently well supplied.

The IJA and IJN had 2,360 engineers in Papua. They constructed 60 miles of motorable road and built 35 bridges. For land transport, the Japanese brought to Papua 2,300 pioneers, 2,000 New Guineans from Rabaul, 2,360 horses, 450 carts, 95 trucks and hundreds of bicycles.

## Air support

The IJN's *11th Air Fleet* (including the famous *Tainan Air Group* in Lae), headquartered at Rabaul, supported land and sea operations in Papua, New Guinea and the Solomon Islands. It maintained bases at Lae, Gasmata, Rabaul, Buka, Buin and briefly at Buna. The *11th Air Fleet* had 95 serviceable combat aircraft (mainly Mitsubishi G4M Bettys and Mitsubishi A6M Zeros) as operations in Papua began. With the American landing at Guadalcanal on 7 August, IJN air was switched to the Solomons, not returning to significant operations in Papua until mid-November. In spite of heavy losses in the Solomons (24 G4M Bettys in the month of September alone), it had then 140 serviceable combat aircraft. On 18 December 1942, the first IJA aircraft, 60 Nakajima Type 1 Oscars of *11th Sentai*, arrived at Rabaul and were soon active over Buna. An army–navy agreement allocated most of the army's effort to Papua, while the navy concentrated on Guadalcanal.

## Health

The Japanese had a long experience of the health problems arising on campaigns in the Asia/Pacific region. Six per cent of the *Nankai Shitai* were medical personnel against four per cent for the Allies. The Japanese had specialists not found among the Allies in Papua: 230 water purification personnel to avert dysentery and a large malaria prevention unit. Until the Japanese sea supply line was cut, quinine and other medical supplies were usually available. All members of the *Nankai Shitai* were inoculated against cholera, plague, typhus, smallpox, typhoid, food poisoning and dysentery.

# ALLIED

## Infantry and artillery

A full-strength Australian brigade in Papua, 2,100 men, was about two-thirds the size of a US regimental combat team. The Australians came from two organizations, the AIF and the Citizen Military Forces (CMF). The AIF members were volunteers, raised when the war began in 1939. They fought in North Africa, Greece, Crete, Syria and Lebanon. With the outbreak of war in the Pacific, they returned to Australia. The CMF was a militia, part conscripted, intended for home defence but obliged to serve in Australian Territories, including Papua and New Guinea.

The United States Army Air Force (USAAF) was defending Port Moresby when the Japanese invaded, but US land forces were not involved in the Kokoda phase of the campaign. US engineers participated in the battle of Milne Bay and, in September 1942, 32nd Infantry Division arrived in Port Moresby. The 32nd, a National Guard division from Michigan and Wisconsin, was one of the first to be sent overseas, arriving in Australia in May 1942. Undermanned, undertrained and underequipped, it performed poorly at first. Its morale, training and equipment, hence combat power, was at the standard of the CMF, but below that of the AIF. One regiment of 41st Division, the 163rd, served at Buna in January 1943.

In small-arms firepower, the Allied infantry had an advantage in jungle fighting. An IJA section had one light machine gun and no submachine guns (the *SNLF* had some), while both Australian and American sections/squads had a light machine gun, sometimes two, and one or two Thompson submachine guns. With heavier weapons, the situation was more often the opposite. On the Kokoda Trail, the Australians initially had no medium or heavy machine guns or mortars. Only briefly at the end of the Japanese advance did they have the support of artillery. At Buna–Gona, the Allies began with no artillery and had only 20 guns by the end.

Captain Thomas Grahamslaw, Australian New Guinea Administrative Unit, briefing Sergeant Major Katue of the Papuan Infantry Battalion. Katue was awarded the Military Medal for scouting the Japanese landing point at Basabua the night after the landing. (Australian War Memorial 127566)

The Papuan Infantry Battalion (PIB) was the first to resist the Japanese invasion. The PIB was a unit of the Australian army, raised in Papua in 1940. Led by Australian and New Zealand officers and non-commissioned officers, it was understrength when, in early 1942, it was sent to patrol the north coast of Papua. It fought on the Kokoda Trail from July to September 1942 and later at Buna–Gona. Sixty PIB recruits were drawn from the Royal Papuan Constabulary, another small Papuan-manned, Australian-officered unit.

## Tanks

Apart from two Japanese tanks, Type 95 Ha-Go, briefly engaged in the battle of Milne Bay, the 19 tanks of the Australian 2/6th Armoured Regiment were the only armour to fight in Papua. The regiment was equipped with M3 Stuart light tanks. Its 44mm hull armour was not proof against Japanese anti-tank guns, but the Stuart was the only tank small and light enough to be transported by sea to Buna. There, equipped with a 37mm M5 gun, it proved its worth as a bunker buster on the battlefield.

*Logistical support*

The Australian New Guinea Administrative Unit provided Papuan carriers for the supply line. Over 10,000 were on hand early in the campaign, three times more carriers than the Japanese could muster. These men forwarded the material necessary to sustain combat and carried wounded to the rear.

The Allies also had the vital advantage of an airlift throughout the campaign. Growing from a dozen to 60 transport aircraft, mainly C-47, each capable of carrying 2,500lb, they made possible the maintenance of the relatively large forces involved in the advance along the Kokoda Trail and the battle of Buna–Gona. Aircraft also delivered almost all of 32nd Division to the north coast of Papua for the battle of Buna–Gona, as well as 14 artillery pieces.

*Air support*

At the beginning of the campaign, the Allied Air Force (AAF; composed of Royal Australian Air Force [RAAF], USAAF and Royal Netherlands Air Force) had 310 serviceable aircraft available for operations in Australia, in Papua and along the sea routes to it. Most were based in Queensland, only refuelling in Port Moresby because of Japanese air raids. As Allied airpower grew and more airfields were built, the majority were stationed at Port Moresby. General George Kenney commanded the AAF. On 5 September, he created a separate 5th Air Force, retaining command of both. The 5th Air Force, which contained both American and Australian squadrons, flew the vast majority of sorties during the Papuan Campaign.

Airpower contributed to the campaign by bombing Rabaul and interdicting Japanese supply at sea. The effort on land was small; Allied air averaged only 15 combat sorties per day over Papua, excluding shipping attacks, until November, and double that thereafter. For what it was worth, the Allies had air superiority over the fighting, but its attempts to interdict supply lines on land and at close battlefield support were not effective primarily because of the difficulty of seeing a target in the jungle. Aerial spotting for artillery at Buna was provided by No 4 Squadron RAAF.

*Health*

The Australians and Americans came to Papua unprepared for the destruction disease would inflict on their armies. In September 1942, there was not one specialist in hygiene among the Allied armies. As a result dysentery took hold of the Australians on the Kokoda Trail, where they evacuated 2,800 sick men from the front line, twice the number the Japanese evacuated. At Milne Bay, the Australians had 5,000 cases of malaria in five months, and two-thirds of all US 32nd Division's casualties at Buna–Gona were to sickness, mainly malaria and dysentery. Post-campaign Allied reports concluded that six months in such an environment as Papua reduces a fighting unit almost to uselessness, even if it was not in combat.

# ORDERS OF BATTLE

## KOKODA TRAIL JULY–NOVEMBER 1942

**Japanese units, *Nankai Shitai*, drawn mainly from 55th Infantry Division**

Commander: Major General Horii Tomitaro
55th Division Headquarters

**144th Infantry Regiment**
1/144th Battalion
2/144th Battalion
3/144th Battalion
**41st Infantry Regiment**
1/41st Battalion
2/41st Battalion
3/41st Battalion
55th Cavalry Regiment (dismounted, one company)
55th Mountain Artillery Regiment (detachment)
55th Engineer Regiment, plus Materials Platoon (part strength)
15th Independent Engineer Regiment (one company)
55th Supply Regiment (one company)
55th Disease Prevention and Water Supply Unit
55th Division Medical Unit (part strength)
55th Division, 1st Field Hospital

**Australian units; termed Maroubra Force until September 1942, then 7th Division**

Commanders from August to November 1942: Brigadier Arnold Potts, Brigadier Selwyn Porter, Brigadier Kenneth Eather, Major General Arthur Allen, Major General George Vasey

**16th Infantry Brigade AIF**
2/1st Infantry Battalion
2/2nd Infantry Battalion
2/3rd Infantry Battalion
**21st Infantry Brigade AIF**
2/14th Infantry Battalion
2/16th Infantry Battalion
2/27th Infantry Battalion
**25th Infantry Brigade AIF**
2/25th Infantry Battalion
2/31st Infantry Battalion
2/33rd Infantry Battalion
**30th Infantry Brigade CMF**
39th Infantry Battalion
53rd Infantry Battalion

3rd Battalion
2/1st Pioneer Battalion
2/6th Independent Company
Papuan Infantry Battalion
Royal Papuan Constabulary
14th Field Regiment
2/5th Field Company, Royal Australian Engineers
2/6th Field Company, Royal Australian Engineers
2/4th Field Ambulance, Australian Army Medical Corps
2/6th Field Ambulance, Australian Army Medical Corps
14th Field Ambulance, Australian Army Medical Corps

## MILNE BAY AUGUST–SEPTEMBER 1942

**Japanese units**

Commanders: Hayashi Shojiro succeeded by Yano Minoru

3rd Kure SNLF
5th Kure SNLF
5th Sasebo SNLF
5th Yokohama SNLF
2nd Tank Regiment (detachment)
19th Base Establishment Unit
8th Signals Unit (detachment)

**Allied units**

Commander: Major General Cyril Clowes

**US**
101st Coast Artillery (Anti-Aircraft) Battalion (one platoon)
C Battery, 104th Coast Artillery (Anti-Aircraft) Battalion
709th Anti-Aircraft Artillery Battery
46th Engineers (one company)
43rd Engineers (less one company)
394th Quartermaster Battalion (one company)
Milne Bay Port Detachment

**Australian**
**7th Infantry Brigade CFM**
9th Infantry Battalion
25th Infantry Battalion
61st Infantry Battalion
**18th Infantry Brigade AIF**
2/9th Infantry Battalion
2/10th Infantry Battalion
2/12th Infantry Battalion
**Artillery**
9th Battery, 2/5th Field Regiment
4th Battery, 101st Anti-Tank Regiment
2/6th Heavy Anti-Aircraft Battery
23rd Heavy Anti-Aircraft Battery (one section)
440th Heavy Anti-Aircraft Gun Station
441st Heavy Anti-Aircraft Gun Station
2/9th Light Anti-Aircraft Battery (less one troop)
**Engineers**
24th Field Company
2/4th Field Company
**Supply and Transport**
25th Company, Australian Army Service Corps
2/6th Company, Australian Army Service Corps
**Medical**
11th Field Ambulance
2/5th Field Ambulance
101st Casualty Clearing Station

# BUNA–GONA NOVEMBER 1942–JANUARY 1943

**Japanese units, 30 November 1942**

Commander: Lieutenant General Tsuyuo Yamagata (from 2 December 1942)

**Buna area**
Replacement Battalion, 144th Regiment (fought separately from 144th Regiment)
3/229th Battalion
2nd Company, 38th Mountain Artillery Regiment
47th Field Anti-aircraft Artillery Battalion (one company)
14th Pioneer Unit
15th Pioneer Unit
5th Yokosuka SNLF

**Sanananda road–Giruwa central area**
South Seas Force Headquarters
5th Sasebo SNLF Detachment
144th Infantry Regiment (main body)
41st Infantry Regiment Detachment
Field Hospital patients (Takeda Unit)
Takasago Volunteer Unit
1st Battalion, 55th Mountain Artillery Regiment
15th Independent Engineer Regiment main strength
19th Independent Engineer Regiment
47th Field Anti-Aircraft Artillery Battalion (main body)
South Seas Force cavalry company
South Seas Force Medical Unit
South Seas Force field hospital
Line-of-communication hospital
Murase Battalion (41st Regiment replacements)
Line-of-communication units
South Seas Force cavalry units
41st Infantry Regiment (less 1st Battalion)
Anchorage Command
17th Army Military Police (detachment)

**Gona area**
Uchida Unit (formed from patients of the line-of-communication hospital)
Nakamura Unit (formed from Takasago volunteers)
Mori Unit (formed from the Disease Prevention and Water Supply Unit)
Soda Unit (Detachment 41st Infantry Regiment)

## Allied units

### US
Buna Force Commander: Lieutenant General Edmund Herring
32nd Division Commander: Major General Edwin Harding, succeeded by Lieutenant General Robert Eichelberger
Headquarters, US I Corps

**32nd Division**
126th Infantry Regimental Combat Team (1st and 2nd Battalions)
3/126th Battalion (detached to 7th Division on Sanananda road)
127th Regimental Combat Team
128th Regimental Combat Team
**41st Division**
163rd Regimental Combat Team
**Artillery**
Battery A, 129th Field Artillery Battalion (one 105mm howitzer)

### Australian
Buna Force Commander: Lieutenant General Edmund Herring
7th Division Commander: Major General George Vasey
Headquarters, 7th Division

2/7th Cavalry Regiment (dismounted)
2/6th Armoured Regiment (composite squadron of 19 M3 Stuart tanks)
**25th Infantry Brigade AIF**
2/25th Infantry Battalion
2/31st Infantry Battalion
2/33rd Infantry Battalion
3rd Battalion (attached)
**Chaforce AIF (composite force formed in September 1942 from elements of 21st Brigade)**
2/14th Infantry Battalion
2/16th Infantry Battalion
2/27th Infantry Battalion
**16th Infantry Brigade AIF**
2/1st Infantry Battalion
2/2nd Infantry Battalion
2/3rd Infantry Battalion
**18th Brigade AIF (initially attached to 32nd Division at Buna)**
2/9th Infantry Battalion
2/10th Infantry Battalion
2/12th Infantry Battalion
**21st Brigade AIF**
2/14th Infantry Battalion
2/16th Infantry Battalion
2/27th Infantry Battalion
39th Infantry Battalion (CMF attached)
**30th Brigade CMF**
36th Infantry Battalion
49th Infantry Battalion
55/53rd Infantry Battalion
**14th Brigade HQ CMF (36th and 55/53rd detached from this brigade for a time)**
2/6th Independent Company attached to Warren Force, 32nd Division
**Artillery**
2/5th Field Regiment (one troop, four 25-pdrs)
2/1st Field Regiment (12 25-pdrs)
13th Field Regiment (one troop, four 4.5in howitzers)
1st Mountain Battery (one troop, three 3.7in howitzers)
**Air**
No 4 Squadron Royal Australian Air Force (two flights)

# OPPOSING PLANS

## JAPANESE

Good plans rely on good intelligence and that the Japanese had. On 13 March 1941, nine months before the Japanese made their move in the Pacific, Major Toyufuku Tetsuo stepped ashore at Port Moresby. He walked around asking questions, bought maps and drove a short distance inland. Toyufuku was an IJA intelligence officer disguised as a seaman of the Japanese merchant ship *Takachiho Maru*. In the years before Pearl Harbor, the Japanese Ministry of Foreign Affairs, in conjunction with the IJA and the IJN, had sent spies to the Pacific, producing reports on each country. Later, Toyufuku, senior intelligence officer of the *Nankai Shitai*, wrote the report on Papua and New Guinea. He found there was no motor road crossing the Owen Stanley Range. There were, however, several routes from the north coast to Port Moresby, the best of which was the one from Sanananda, near Buna. Other IJA officers in disguise took grass samples to see if fodder was available for the horse-reliant Japanese army. Reports covered roads, bridges, rainfall, available food and the prevalence of malaria.

The IJA collected maps pre-war, some obtained in Australia. In June 1942, Prince Takeda Tsuneyoshi of IHQ staff gave 'an English explorer's map' of Papua to *17th Army* staff prior to their leaving Japan for Rabaul. The IJN charts of the Solomon and Coral Seas, superior to those of the Allies, were German. They were drawn up by the Imperial German Navy when New Guinea was a colony of the German Empire before World War I. In 1941, Japanese naval officers improved on their charts, including charting the anchorage at Basabua, the one used for the invasion of Papua.

The Japanese studies on which the plan to invade Papua was based emphasized that terrain, climate and maintaining the health of their troops would all be formidable obstacles. They could hardly have chosen a more comfortless location for a campaign. With peaks up to 13,000ft, the Owen Stanley Range runs as a backbone down the length of Papua. From it, to north and south, flow fast rivers and creeks. At the malarial coasts – Buna was a hyperendemic area – the rivers slow to wide swamps, with few flat, dry areas. Over all this is a cover of forest and jungle, with patches of sharp 4–6ft-high kunai grass. Rainfall can be torrential, 10in a day in the wet season from October to March.

There was an element of caution in the plan. Colonel Yokoyama Yosuke led an 'advanced force' to Papua, and was to report to Rabaul if he found some

Japanese bombing raid on Port Moresby, March 1942. The target was a convoy recently arrived from Queensland. (Australian War Memorial P02018.068)

reason why the march over the Owen Stanley Range was not possible. This force, with fewer fighting troops but a lot of specialists, landed three weeks before the main body to fortify the new Buna base, set up a supply line as far forward as Kokoda, build an airfield, lengthen the motorable part of the Sanananda road and build bridges. Yokoyama gave an affirmative report, the route was practical and the main body sailed from Rabaul on 12 August 1942.

No roads connected the strategic points in Papua: Port Moresby, Buna and Milne Bay. With mountainous jungle in between, each was, in a sense, an island. An army on each 'island' could not, the Allies believed, move from one to another unless by air or by sea. Movement of any large body of troops by land would encounter insuperable supply problems. The Japanese saw it differently, intending to cross from one 'island' to another by land, along the Kokoda Trail. This was their main effort. It was to be supported by a landing on the eastern tip of Papua, at Milne Bay, a few weeks after the main body arrived. In fact, the nearby island of Samarai was their first choice for this operation, but when they discovered in July that the Allies were constructing three airstrips at Milne Bay, Lieutenant General Hyakutake Harukichi decided that Milne Bay would be the better option.

The importance of Milne Bay was that it had flat, dry land suitable for airstrips close to the coast. Airfields needed to be near the sea in Papua, in common with other places in the Pacific, as only sea transport could supply the heavy and bulky requirements, mainly fuel and bombs, that an airfield containing several squadrons constantly consumes. Inland airstrips like that at Kokoda could never become large air bases. From Milne Bay, aircraft could dominate the Coral Sea to the south towards Queensland, and east across the Solomon Sea to the Solomon Islands. Moreover, aircraft from Milne Bay could attack Port Moresby without the disadvantage of flying through the difficult weather in the Owen Stanley Range. Milne Bay was also to be a staging point for coastal Daihatsu barges, which the Japanese intended to use for a second prong to their offensive to capture Port Moresby. Covered by aircraft operating from the bay, a force of several thousand would pass through the China Strait, hop along the south coast of Papua at night, 200 miles, arriving in Port Moresby at the same time as the *Nankai Shitai* coming from the Kokoda Trail.

# ALLIED

Though it was a territory of Australia, by the end of 1941 the IJA and IJN knew as much, if not more, about Papua than did the Australian armed forces. The Australian Directorate of Naval Intelligence and the Commonwealth Investigation Branch warned the government pre-war that Japanese spies were active in Papua, but nothing was done.

That Papua might become a battlefield only became apparent to the Australians when the Japanese took Rabaul in January 1942. The Coral Sea battle made plain that that was indeed the Japanese intention. Then, in June, Allied codebreakers learned that the result of the Coral Sea had not deterred the Japanese; they were considering trying again. All that had been done for the defence of Papua was to place a brigade-sized garrison in Port Moresby, construct four airfields there and improve warehousing and jetties. There were also 105 men of the PIB in small observation groups along 50 miles of the north coast of Papua. On 9 June, MacArthur wrote to Blamey asking what else was being done. This resulted, eventually, in action. The 39th Battalion, part of the Port Moresby garrison, was to occupy Kokoda, company by company over several weeks. The first company, marching along the Kokoda Trail which began at Ower's Corner, arrived at Kokoda on 14 July, a week before the Japanese landed in Papua. As a measure of the lack of preparedness, maps of Papua of military use hardly existed. When Major General Cyril Clowes arrived to take command at Milne Bay in July, he had no maps at all; as Australians marched north along the Kokoda Trail in September and October, they had to make maps themselves as they went along.

As a result of the engineers' visit to Dobodura, plans were made to build a base there. On 17 July, orders were issued for the build-up of a garrison, engineers, communications and anti-aircraft units to move to Dobodura by sea from Milne Bay and by air from Port Moresby. The first units would arrive on 31 July and the force was to be in place and complete 25 days later. Before the move began, intelligence advised that a large build-up of Japanese shipping in Rabaul may indicate they were moving on Buna too. On 21 July, before any important acceleration of the Allied plan was possible, the Japanese landed at Basabua, near Buna. Papua, which was to have served as the base for an Allied offensive directed at Salamaua and Lae, had now to be defended.

# THE CAMPAIGN

## THE JAPANESE ADVANCE ON THE KOKODA TRAIL

Under *15 Independent Engineer Regiment (IER)* commander Colonel Yokoyama Yosuke, the advanced party of the *Nankai Shitai*, 4,000 men, sailed from Rabaul to Basabua in two convoys, each of two transports with escorts. They disembarked on 21 and 29 July 1942 at the cost of one vessel, *Ayatozan Maru*, sunk by air attack after unloading. Their tasks were to improve the basic airstrip near Buna, build defences for the new base and establish a supply line to Kokoda for the main body.

The landing at Basabua was unopposed. A PIB platoon was close enough to observe the landing. It did not engage but left to report to its commander, Major William Watson, at Awala. The Australians manning the Buna wireless station also left when they learned of the Japanese presence. The first Japanese departure from the anchorage was a company of *1/144th Battalion*. One hundred and thirty-five men, under Captain Ogawa Tetsuo, boarded trucks at 1630hrs on 21 July. Ogawa also took along bicycles, a platoon of the battalion gun company with one 70mm gun, a platoon of the battalion's machine gun company and one engineer platoon carrying rubber boats. He was accompanied by local Orokaiva guides. Ogawa's advanced guard, 230 men, did all the fighting against the Papuans and Australians up to and including the first Kokoda engagement on 29 July 1942.

The advance was rapid as the road towards Kokoda was suitable for motor vehicles for 30 miles, almost to Awala. The first engagement occurred there two days after the landing, when 37 men of the PIB under Lieutenant John Chalk fired on the Japanese, then retreated. Later that day, a platoon of 39th Battalion, ordered forward from Kokoda upon news of the Japanese landing, engaged them farther to the west.

Bridge across the Kumusi River at Wairopi constructed by Australian engineers. (Australian War Memorial 013755)

# Fighting on the Kokoda Trail, July–November 1942

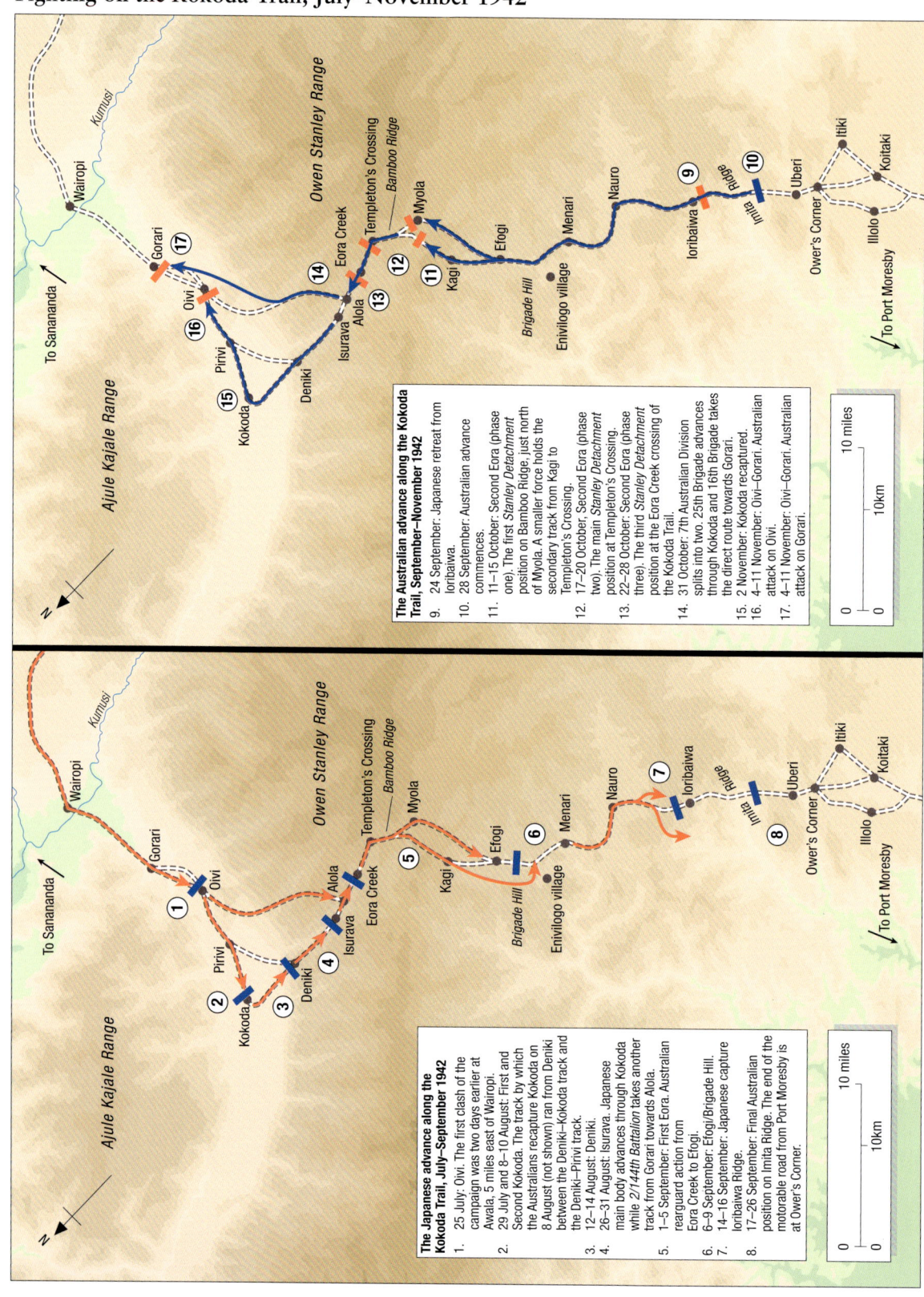

The Australians demolished the bridge across the Kumusi River at Wairopi and, on 24 July, fire was exchanged across the river. The Australians and Papuans, by now 100 strong, fell back to Gorari where, on 25 July, they ambushed the Japanese, killing two men.

Since the Japanese landing, the commander of the Australian/Papuan force, Colonel William Owen, had attempted to assemble the 300 available men from his 39th Battalion, the Royal Papuan Constabulary (RPC) and the PIB. At Oivi, when he had half of them, 60 Papuans and 90 Australians, he made the first serious effort to contest the advance. The Japanese attack, again led by Orokaiva guides, almost encircled the defenders who fought on until the evening then escaped.

The arrival of the Japanese intruded into tribal politics. Many Orokaiva volunteered as armed scouts for the Japanese. Others, such as the Bininderi and Koiari, were employed by the Australian administration, and sided with Australia. Others had no reason to favour either side. Of necessity, it was more important for them to consider the effect of the arrival of the Japanese on the web of political relations between tribes. Some calculated it was in their interest to support the Japanese, especially if a local enemy had thrown in their lot with the Australians.

## First Kokoda

After Oivi, the Japanese advanced on Kokoda. Here the most important terrain feature was the airstrip west of the steep-sided, flat-topped ridge on which sat the Kokoda Government Station, not far west of Kokoda village. The army that held the strip could fly in reinforcements while denying the same to the enemy. The Japanese planned to use the Kokoda strip for air movement and supply as the Australians later did, but the allocation of Japanese air assets to the Guadalcanal campaign from the end of August prevented this.

The defenders held the flat-topped ridge. There were 148 men in total: 111 39th Battalion, 20 PIB, 9 RPC and minor detachments from the Australian New Guinea Administrative Unit (ANGAU) and 30th Brigade. Ogawa's force after casualties was over 200 strong.

Soldiers of *1/144th Battalion* resting near Kokoda. (144th Infantry Regiment Association)

**FIRST CONTACT, PAPUANS AT AWALA, 23 JULY 1942 (PP. 26–27)**

Lieutenant John Chalk **(1)** was an officer of the Papuan Infantry Battalion. Born in Brisbane, the 26 year old commanded at the Awala ambush, the first engagement of the Papuan Campaign. Chalk had scouts keeping track of the Japanese advance from the coast when he received a five-word order from Major William Watson, commander of the PIB and headquartered at Awala. Written on cardboard, the order stated, 'You will engage the enemy.'

Chalk chose a position with a good field of fire **(2)**. He placed his men on a hill slope 1,000 yards east of Awala (5 miles east of Wairopi) and overlooking the Sanananda road along which the Japanese advanced. To his front was a vegetable garden.

The PIB's task on the north coast of Papua was to observe and report on any Japanese landing. There were 120 of the battalion spread throughout the region when the Japanese landed near Buna on 21 July 1942. Watson gathered 37 of them to place under Chalk's command **(3)**.

One or two Type 92 70mm guns **(4)** belonged to each Japanese infantry battalion. The Type 92 was a small howitzer which could also be used in direct fire mode. It had an effective range of 3,000 yards, fired six rounds per minute and weighed 500lb. It could be taken apart and carried by infantry, as it was along the Kokoda Trail.

Like almost all members of *144th Regiment*, 27-year-old Captain Ogawa Tetsuo **(5)** was from the mountainous Kochi Prefecture in southern Shikoku. His force was the first to leave the anchorage after the Japanese invasion force arrived on 21 July. He commanded at all engagements up to and including First Kokoda on 29 July, where he was killed.

Ogawa's 230-man force included his own *1st Company* **(6)**, a platoon of the battalion's gun company with one 70mm gun, a platoon of the machine gun company and an engineer platoon.

The Japanese attacked from the north at 0230hrs on 29 July. An hour later, with Colonel Owen fatally wounded, the order to withdraw was given. Ogawa, too, was killed. The Japanese may have seen two Australian aircraft that circled Kokoda on 29 July but did not land. They contained 30 men of 49th Battalion. The rest of the company was sitting by the runway at Seven Mile strip at Port Moresby. The Australians intended to send a company a day by air to Kokoda, but Ogawa's attack forestalled this.

## Second Kokoda

The Australians retreated along the Kokoda Trail into the Owen Stanley Range to Deniki, which overlooked Kokoda. For a week, the Japanese awaited the rest of *1/144th Battalion*. A company of engineers from *15 IER* arrived to improve the route from Oivi to Kokoda as *15 Naval Pioneers* (NP) brought supplies to Kokoda. The full strength of *1/144th* was not assembled until 7 August. Its commander, Lieutenant Colonel Tsukamoto Hatsuo, advanced on Deniki the next day to make a battalion attack. Instead, he bumped into Australians advancing in the other direction for, on the same day Tsukamoto advanced, so did his enemy. Maroubra Force, the new code name for the Australian/Papuan force, counter-attacked to recapture Kokoda under its new commander Major Allan Cameron.

Tsukamoto had 522 of *1/144th Battalion* and two platoons, 120 men, of *15 IER*. Adding small signals and medical detachments and not counting a handful of Orokaiva, there were 660 Japanese. The 39th's B Company, which Cameron thought should be disbanded due to its poor behaviour at First Kokoda where 27 men deserted, was sent back to Eora. Cameron's force was 430 strong excluding his reserve company, which

Kokoda from the air, with the foothills of the Owen Stanley Range in the background. The Sanananda road enters from bottom left (east). The Australian position for First Kokoda was on the high ground near the word 'village'. (Australian War Memorial 128400)

Japanese transporting equipment by cart in Papua. Each battalion brought 50 carts, which proved useful until the foothills of the Owen Stanley Range were reached. (144th Infantry Regiment Association)

was not engaged. His plan was to re-occupy Kokoda Government Station, allowing reinforcements to arrive by air. He sent four companies by three routes. One rifle company, with Cameron and his headquarters company, was on the left, heading directly down the Trail towards Kokoda. These met Tsukamoto coming the other way. Another company was to Cameron's right and another went to the Australian far right, to the Kokoda–Oivi track junction at Pirivi, to prevent Japanese reinforcements arriving at Kokoda. Here at Pirivi, the company, with 21 PIB attached, encountered two platoons of *15 IER* engaged in bridge construction. The Australians fought them until dark, killing six and wounding 16, then withdrew to Deniki.

The company in the Australian centre entered Kokoda Station along an unguarded track, then dug in there. The leftmost of the Australian three-pronged attack met with the Japanese advanced guard a mile from Deniki. Cameron drove it back until he met the main body of *1/144th*. Tsukamoto, unsure what this unexpected meeting portended, probed the Australians through the afternoon until the latter withdrew to Deniki. Tsukamoto followed and arrived in Deniki on the evening of 8 August when he learned Kokoda Station in his rear had been retaken by the Australians.

Tsukamoto sent back a company, a machine gun company platoon and a battalion gun. They attacked that night and proved inadequate to the task. The following day, 9 August, short of ammunition and food, with no reinforcements arriving by air owing to a lack of communication with Port Moresby, the Australian company evacuated Kokoda. Soon, all of Maroubra Force was back where it had begun, holding Deniki, and Tsukamoto was able to continue with his delayed plan to attack it.

## *Deniki*

On 12 August, Tsukamoto restarted his attack on Deniki with a bombardment by the 70mm battalion gun. He had 450 men, Cameron had 470. The Japanese scouted the Australian position on 13 August, then attacked with two companies, but by nightfall, little ground had been gained. This was not a charge with fixed bayonets – only two Japanese were killed. It was a careful movement by platoons inching their way forward. The Japanese were wary of taking unnecessary casualties among, at this stage of the war, their well-trained and combat-wise infantry. They believed that an enemy could often be 'worried' out of his position by methodical, persistent pressure. Tsukamoto harassed the Australians again that night and attacked the next day to find that the worrying had worked – the Australians were gone.

Japanese battle casualties thus far in the campaign were 50 killed and 87 wounded. Australian and Papuan casualties were 42 killed and 34 wounded.

## *Isurava*

The Australians retreated to Isurava, where a large reinforcement joined them. Since the Japanese landing in Papua, veteran AIF troops had been despatched to Port Moresby, then sent north along the Kokoda Trail, arriving at Isurava late in August. Some AIF might have been sent earlier, but to delay the inevitable deterioration in health troops suffered in Papua, they were retained in Australia until it was clear that that the Japanese objective was Port Moresby. The initial Allied view was that the Japanese may only be interested in establishing a base at Buna, protecting it with a covering force at Kokoda. Once it was apparent Port Moresby was their objective, Australian reinforcements poured in.

Maroubra Force now consisted of four infantry battalions, a headquarters, detachments of ANGAU, PIB, RPC and a medical team, totalling 2,292 men. The new commander was Brigadier Arnold Potts, a veteran of Gallipoli and the Western Front in World War I and of Syria in the present war.

The main body of the *Nankai Shitai*, which landed near Buna from 19 to 21 August, was also present with its commander, Major General Horii Tomitaro. Anxious to destroy the Australians before they retreated farther into the mountains, he force-marched the men, with 60lb packs, 70 miles from the north coast to Isurava. One-quarter fell out along the way, not arriving in time for the battle.

With the three battalions of *144th Regiment* providing 1,500 men, the total Japanese force engaged from 27 August, allowing for those who had fallen out during the forced march, was 2,130. On 30 August, the last of four days' fighting, the gun company of *144th Regiment* and one more company of the mountain artillery battalion arrived, bringing Japanese strength to 2,400 men. At Deniki, 3 miles behind the front line, Horii stationed a reinforced battalion group of 1,100 men, built around *2/41st Battalion*. Once *144th Regiment* won the battle, *2/41st Regiment* would be fresh for the pursuit.

The Isurava position faced north towards Kokoda on both sides of a steep gorge, at the bottom of which Eora Creek ran towards Kokoda. On the west side of the gorge, where the Kokoda Trail was, the Australians dug in on the crest of a slope leading down to Front Creek, which ran at a right angle to Eora Creek. However, this position was overlooked to the north by a ridge which gave the Japanese guns, two at first, later six, an opportunity for direct fire onto the Australians. A second disadvantage of the position was a track junction at Alola, immediately to the rear of the Australians on the west side of the gorge. A track on the east side of the gorge led to Alola, offering an alternative approach into the Australian rear. The 53rd Battalion was placed on the eastern slope to cover this track. The rest of Maroubra Force deployed on the west side.

Horii's plan was a double envelopment. The *1/144th Battalion* was to pin the Australians (2/14th and 39th Battalions) on Front Creek while *2/144th Battalion*, with one gun, east of the gorge, went around the Australian right flank to capture Alola. After giving these two attacks time to draw in Australian reserves, *3/144th Battalion* would swing around the Australian left, trapping the whole force. The plan did not work. Not only did the double envelopment fail, but an additional two days' fighting was needed to dislodge the enemy. The determination of the Australians accounts for one of these days and Japanese errors for the other.

Looking first at events east of Eora gorge, *2/144th* arrived on 26 August too exhausted by the forced march to attack. Its one achievement was to find a position from which the battalion gun and the machine gun company could fire across to the western side of the gorge, inflicting casualties on Maroubra Force Headquarters (MFHQ) and 2/4th Field Ambulance.

Looking north from the Australian position on the left bank of the Eora gorge at Isurava. The nearest of two ridges on the left is where the Japanese placed their artillery. The main Japanese attack came towards the camera on the left-hand slope, where the Kokoda Trail is, while *2/144th Battalion* attacked along the right-hand slope. The memorial commemorates all Australians and Papuans who fought on the Kokoda Trail. (Author's Collection)

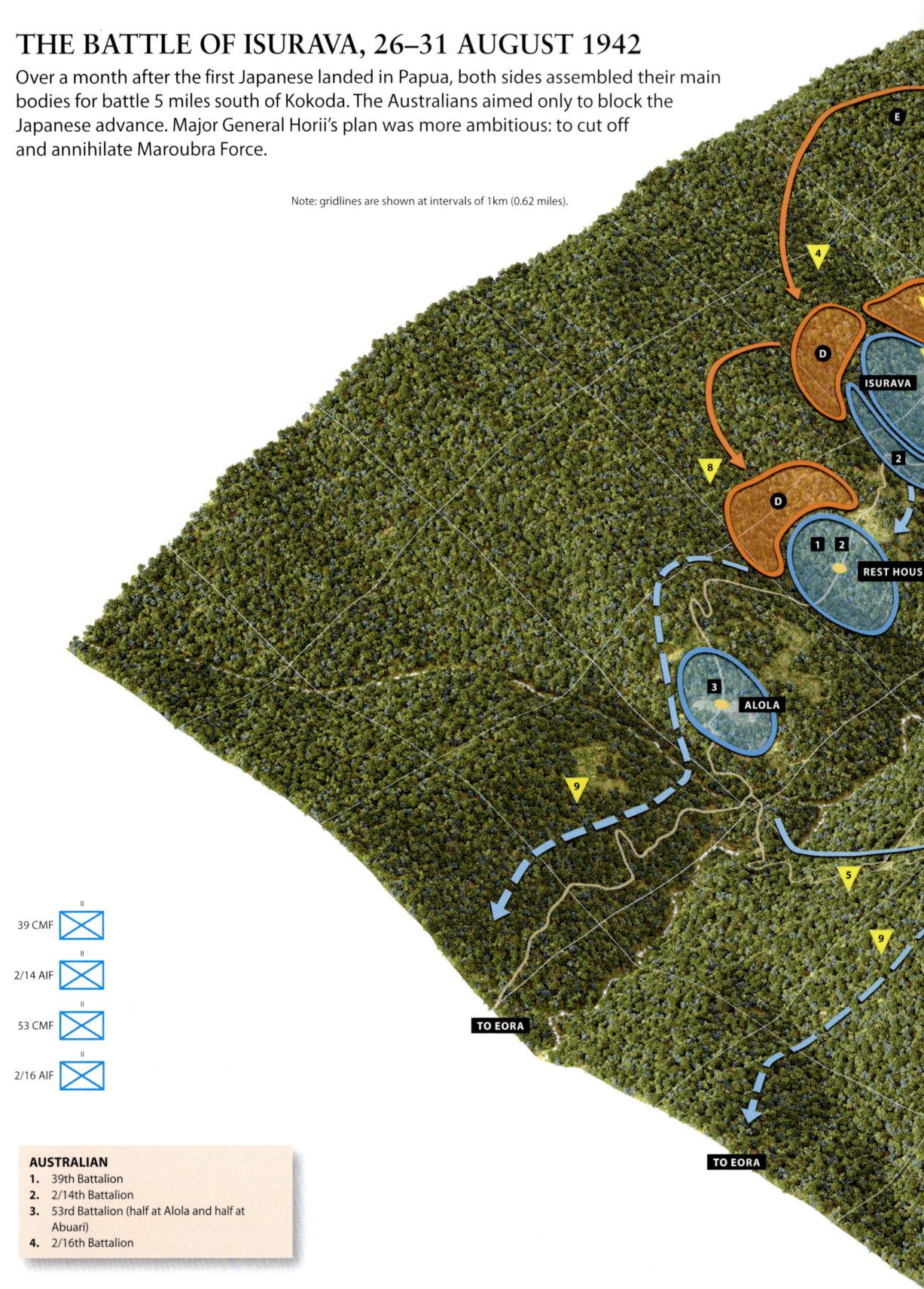

# THE BATTLE OF ISURAVA, 26–31 AUGUST 1942

Over a month after the first Japanese landed in Papua, both sides assembled their main bodies for battle 5 miles south of Kokoda. The Australians aimed only to block the Japanese advance. Major General Horii's plan was more ambitious: to cut off and annihilate Maroubra Force.

Note: gridlines are shown at intervals of 1km (0.62 miles).

**AUSTRALIAN**
1. 39th Battalion
2. 2/14th Battalion
3. 53rd Battalion (half at Alola and half at Abuari)
4. 2/16th Battalion

## JAPANESE

A. *2/41st Battalion*
B. *1/144th Battalion*
C. *2/144th Battalion*
D. *3/144th Battalion*
E. Two guns (battalion gun of *1/144th* and mountain gun from *55th Mountain Artillery Regiment*) until 30 August. Four more guns arrive on 30 August (two from *55th Mountain Artillery Regiment* and two from the *144th*'s regimental gun company). One battalion gun was forward with *1/144th* and one with *2/144th*

## EVENTS

**1.** 26 August: Patrols from the Japanese *1/144th Battalion* locate the Australian position and shell 39th Battalion.

**2.** 27 August: *1/144th Battalion* attacks the 39th Battalion at Isurava as it is being reinforced by 2/14th Battalion. Late on 28 August the fresh 2/14th moves into 39th Battalion position while the half strength 39th retires to 2/14th position.

**3.** 27 August: *2/144th Battalion*, supported by its battalion gun, attacks half of 53rd Battalion.

**4.** 28 August: *3/144th Battalion* moves out to flank 2/14th Battalion.

**5.** 28 August: *2/144th Battalion* becomes lost for the day searching for, but not finding, a way to flank 53rd Battalion to the east (not shown). On 29 August, the Australian 2/16th Battalion arrives to relieve 53rd Battalion.

**6.** 29 August: During a 2/14th counter-attack, Private Bruce Kingsbury attacks the headquarters of *No 1 Company 1/144th*, eliminating it. Kingsbury is killed soon after. He is awarded a Victoria Cross for this action.

**7.** 29 August: Under attack from *3/144th Battalion*, the Australians west of Eora Creek withdraw to the Rest House.

**8.** 30 August: *3/144th Battalion* attacks the Australian positions at the Rest House.

**9.** 31 August: The Australians withdraw from the Rest House, Abuari and Alola.

**10.** 31 August: Horii's reserve, the *2/41st Battalion*, circle to the west (not shown) in an attempt to get behind the Australians. It becomes lost in the jungle, emerging at Rest House hours after the Australians had left the battlefield.

The next day, 53rd Battalion halted *2/144th*'s advance towards Alola. The 53rd has a poor reputation as a result of its performance at Isurava, but on that day, it did its job. Major Horie Masao, the commander of *2/144th*, was convinced his opponents were so strong that another frontal attack would not work; a flank march was called for. In attempting it, *2/144th* became lost in thick jungle, failing to make contact with the enemy. On 29 August, *2/144th* found the eastern track again and struck a major blow towards Alola. At this point, the 53rd fell apart. According to a report, one company 'appears to have dissolved soon after contact was made'. Potts shifted his reserve, two companies of 2/16th, east across the creek. They barely managed to stop the Japanese cutting in behind Maroubra Force to Alola.

West of Eora gorge on 26 August, *1/144th* patrols found the extent of the Australian position enabling their artillery to shell 39th Battalion. The next day, *1/144th* advanced to make contact with the Australians on a two-company front directly south along the Kokoda Trail. One infantry company was held in reserve. Some progress was made.

On 28 August, the day *2/144th* became lost east of the Eora gorge, there was also a lull on the western side. Horii decided to give *2/144th* one more day to take Alola, so he postponed the *3/144th*'s trapping manoeuvre. He had by now realized that the Australians were at least triple the strength he had expected.

Soon after midnight on 28 August, leaving a company with *1/144th*, the rest of *3/144th* commenced its move to the high ground on the Australian left-rear. As with *2/144th* across the valley, it soon became lost, bumping into the western flank of the Australians. The Japanese backed off and made a wider flanking move. By dawn, one company was where it wanted to be and, with artillery support, commenced its attack against 2/14th Battalion, but achieved nothing. Meanwhile, *1/144th*, facing Isurava from the north along Front Creek, briefly broke into the Australian position, but it was ejected by a counter-attack, taking heavy losses. Thereafter, *1/144th*, having shot its bolt, made no contribution to the battle.

Typical log bridge on the Kokoda Trail, as they are now and were in 1942. Every wet season, they are washed away and rebuilt. Both Australians and Japanese had to manhandle all heavy equipment over such bridges several times each day. (Edward Reeves/Alamy Stock Photo)

By last light on 29 August, all Australian reserves were committed. During the night, Potts ordered a withdrawal to Isurava Rest House, half a mile south. The withdrawal was completed without disruption. Potts sent a succinct situation report to Rowell at NGF: 'Enemy aggressive and successful to date.'

On 30 August, the Australians were in the new position. Two battalions, 39th and 2/14th, blocked the Trail with two companies of 2/16th behind them and the remainder of 2/16th east of the gorge. They came under a strengthened artillery bombardment. Prior to this, only the battalion gun of *1/144th* and one mountain gun fired on them, but now two more 75mm guns of the mountain artillery arrived, together with the *144th*'s regimental gun company (RGC). There were now eight guns firing on the Australians from a range of a mile or less. Six were on the same ridge where the Japanese first set up their artillery, one was east of the gorge with *2/144th* and one went forward in close support of *1/144th*.

During the night, *3/144th* moved south again, through the jungle along the high ground west of Isurava Rest House, this time with no loss of direction. Having found the Australians, *3/144th*'s signallers contacted the guns to bring fire onto Rest House while the battalion's machine gun company was placed to overlook it. The artillery bombardment, together with the machine gun fire, contributed to Pott's decision to order a retreat. As it began, a company of *3/144th* attacked down the hill towards the Australians. A company of 2/14th was ordered to put in a counter-attack to relieve the pressure. The Australian counter-attack went in the wrong direction, south instead of west, scattering and causing casualties to 2/14th's headquarters, then gathering on the track to retreat. Battalion commander Lieutenant Colonel Arthur Key and his staff were dispersed. Key was later captured and executed. From the moment 2/14th's headquarters was scattered by friendly fire, the Australian withdrawal to Eora village became disorderly.

At about the same moment, unaware the Australians were retreating, Horii felt he could no longer afford to keep *2/41st* fresh for the pursuit. He ordered it to make a wide sweep up to the heights on the Australian left and cut the Trail deep in their rear. In a mistake to be seen again and again in jungle fighting in Papua, the battalion left the Trail and was lost for 15 hours, emerging on the Trail north of Isurava Rest House early in the morning of 31 August to discover the Australians long gone.

Ninety-nine Australians were killed and 111 wounded. Japanese infantry losses were 130 dead and 226 wounded. The artillery suffered no loss. Isurava proved to be one fight too many for *1/144th*, having now lost one-third of the men with which it had landed in Papua and half the number with which it had left Japan eight months earlier. No replacements had arrived. Horii had seen the battalion perform poorly at Isurava and relegated it to transport duties, carrying wounded and supplies. It was not committed to battle again for two months.

Potts was fortunate that Horii mishandled the action. Had *2/144th* been as aggressive as *3/144th* and had they both, as well as *2/41st*, not become lost in the jungle, it is difficult to see how Potts could have escaped with a less severe defeat than that administered to him at Efogi a week later. At Isurava, Horii defeated Maroubra Force, but failed to destroy it. The feeling among Japanese officers was summed up by Major Koiwai Mitsuo, commander of *2/41st*: 'We missed a great prize.'

# GUADALCANAL

As Horii was making a mess of his opportunity to destroy the Australians at Isurava, he received an order from Hyakutake, the importance of which can hardly be overestimated: the offensive to Port Moresby was postponed.

On 7 August, US Marines landed at Guadalcanal and Tulagi, taking from the Japanese an airfield they were constructing there. IHQ in Tokyo decided that until Guadalcanal was recovered, no attack on Port Moresby should be made. They directed the movement of IJA assets, those Horii expected would reinforce him, to Guadalcanal. The formations which would have made an attack on Port Moresby viable: the *Kawaguchi Detachment* in the Palau Islands, the *Aoba Detachment* in the Philippines and the *Ichiki Detachment* at Guam, over 7,000 men, went to Guadalcanal instead of Papua. The IJN, which was providing all air support for the theatre, also abandoned Papua for three months to concentrate its efforts on Guadalcanal. A week after the Marine landing, Horii, still at Rabaul, was warned unofficially that his attack on Port Moresby might be held up by Guadalcanal. The actual order confirming this came to him during Isurava.

A new order instructed Horii to secure an advanced location with a lesser force, short of Port Moresby, but close enough to threaten it. His main body was to stay north of the Owen Stanley Range, where it could be more easily supplied while waiting for the advance to Port Moresby to resume, and where elements could be extracted by sea from Buna, should that be required. Thus, instead of sending at least 8,000 fighting troops along the Kokoda Trail to combine outside Port Moresby with an amphibious landing launched from Milne Bay, Horii sent forward just four already weakened infantry battalions, two engineer companies and a reduced artillery battalion. These 3,400 men advanced beyond Isurava to secure a position on the southern slopes of the mountains from which a future attack on Port Moresby could be mounted. This force achieved its aim, but no new order from Rabaul for Horii to capture Port Moresby ever arrived.

# MILNE BAY

The other event occurring during the battle of Isurava, which also made it unlikely the attack on Port Moresby would take place, was the battle of Milne Bay. On 22 June 1942, the Allies began constructing three airstrips there, on the eastern tip of Papua. The first aircraft landed on 22 July. On 3 August, Japanese air reconnaissance discovered the activity at Milne Bay. Hyakutake had previously planned to capture nearby Samari Island, construct an airstrip there and use it as a staging point for the coastal barge advance to Port Moresby to coincide with the advance along the Kokoda Trail. He saw that Milne Bay would do just as well for that task, and unless it was taken, the shipping for the *Nankai Shitai* from Rabaul to Buna would be threatened by Allied air attack from the new Milne Bay airfields. The IJN agreed. No sea movement would be possible around the eastern end of Papua towards Port Moresby with Allied aircraft operating from Milne Bay. When Vice Admiral Mikawa Gunichi sank the Allied cruiser squadron off Savo Island, Guadalcanal (8–9 August), this persuaded IHQ that the time was right. Without cruiser cover, the USN carriers were believed to be very unlikely to venture into the Coral Sea or the Solomon Sea to interrupt a landing to capture Milne Bay.

# The battle of Milne Bay, 25 August–6 September 1942

Major General Cyril Clowes. Clowes commanded Milne Force during the battle of Milne Bay. (HUM Images/ Universal Images Group via Getty Images)

As IJA formations were not yet available but naval infantry were, the IJA handed over the operation to *8th Fleet* Headquarters, also in Rabaul. It was believed there was less than a battalion of Allied troops at Milne Bay, information which was accurate to 11 July, but seriously inaccurate thereafter. There were in fact over 9,000 Australians and Americans present, half of them infantry, with a battery of field artillery. The IJN had on hand 2,400 *SNLF* troops and navy pioneers, which, if the intelligence was correct, would be sufficient.

Just as the Japanese feared an Allied landing at their Buna base and kept a strong garrison there, so Blamey and MacArthur feared a Japanese landing at Milne Bay. A Japanese airfield there would bring Allied airfields and ports in northern Queensland within range of Japanese bombers, as well as threatening shipping on the route from the eastern coast of Australia to Port Moresby, shipping on which all operations in Papua depended. Codebreakers in Melbourne confirmed MacArthur's fear with intelligence about Japanese plans. Reinforcements were quickly sent to Milne Bay, but the Japanese failed to notice.

At 0830hrs on 24 August, the expected Japanese convoy was sighted by an RAAF Hudson 110 miles north-east of Milne Bay: two light cruisers, three destroyers, two transports and two subchasers. Reports of a second convoy, seven barges, which had sailed from Buna carrying another *SNLF* group, were also received. In response to this second sighting, 12 RAAF Kittyhawks scrambled from Milne Bay at 1200hrs. The barges were seen beached at Goodenough Island, where the 357 men of *5th Sasebo SNLF*, led by Commander Tsukioka Torashigo, had gone ashore for the night. They intended to land at Taupota, 5 miles north of Milne Bay, attacking the Allies in the rear at the same time as the main landing took place. The Australian pilots strafed the barges, destroying all and stranding *5th Sasebo*. An air attack on the main convoy failed. Japanese aircraft attacked Milne Bay at the

Pilots of the *Tainan Air Group* in Lae, 1942. Flying A6M Zeros, the *Tainan Air Group* flew missions in support of the Japanese landing at Milne Bay. (Pictures from History/ Universal Images Group via Getty Images)

same time, one of the last significant IJN air operations in Papua until November.

At 2230hrs on 25 August, *809 SNLF* and *362 NP* landed at Wahahuba on the northern shore of the bay. With them were two light tanks, three 37mm guns, two flamethrowers and two 70mm infantry guns.

Due to an error in navigation, and a clash with Australians moving along the coast in small vessels at night, the Japanese came ashore 6 miles east of Rabi, where they had intended to land, dashing their hopes of a surprise attack. This placed them 8 miles from No 3 Strip and 12 miles from No 1 Strip, which was the only operational airfield at that time.

At dawn on 26 August, Kittyhawks from Nos 75 and 76 Squadrons RAAF attacked the Japanese landing area, destroying barges and supply dumps.

Everything that could have gone wrong for the Japanese did go wrong. The force landed in the wrong place; one prong of the attack, which was to have landed at Taupota, was stranded at Goodenough Island; then their barges were sunk, taking away the option to outflank the Australians along the northern shore of Milne Bay at night. Communications with Buna and Rabaul also failed and as a result the IJN did not know when there was a break in the persistent low clouds and heavy rain such that air support might be effective. The *4th Fleet* later estimated that only one in four sorties to Milne Bay from Buna strip (operational from 14 August), Lae and Gasmata were of any value. In contrast, the RAAF, with No 1 Strip only minutes away, could attack when there was a short break in the cloud and rain. The appalling weather during the battle – it rained heavily every day – also inhibited land movement on the one track along the north shore of the bay. This track, boggy and hemmed in by the bay to the south and mountains to the north, was the only avenue of advance open to the Japanese. Nevertheless, they set off with the tanks, driving back elements of 61st Battalion to KB Mission.

Major General Cyril Clowes, commander of Milne Force, had planned to defend with his untried and not well-trained militia brigade (three battalions), keeping his AIF brigade (three battalions) to counter-attack when the moment was right. However, the deteriorating situation, and news that tanks were with the Japanese, forced him to commit 2/10th, which relieved the 61st Battalion, digging in at KB Mission in all-round defence. Attacked on the night of 27/28 August, 2/10th had no effective anti-tank weapons (humidity prevented sticky bombs attaching to the tanks) to stop the Japanese tanks penetrating the perimeter. The coast track was awash, thwarting an

No 76 Squadron Kittyhawk, September 1942. P-40 Kittyhawks of Nos 75 and 76 Squadrons, flying from No 1 Strip at Milne Bay, only minutes from the scene of battle, flew over 300 sorties against the Japanese landing. (Australian War Memorial 026647)

Australian infantry patrol in mud at Milne Bay. (Australian War Memorial 013335)

Bogged Type 95 Ha-Go Japanese tanks at Milne Bay. The coastal track on the north side of Milne Bay was a foot deep in mud for most of the battle. Neither Japanese tanks nor any other wheeled or tracked vehicles could get far along it. The tanks bogged 5 miles from the landing place. (Keystone/Getty Images)

United States engineers, Milne Bay, August 1942. (Australian War Memorial 148941)

effort to bring 6-pdr anti-tank guns forward. As Clowes explained to Rowell in Port Moresby, 'Country very difficult here, only track 2–3 feet deep in mud.'

Roughly handled in their first encounter with Japanese troops, the Middle East veterans' commander, Lieutenant Colonel James Dobbs, ordered 2/10th to retreat to Motieau Creek. The *SNLF* outflanked that position, so he withdrew again to Gama River where a Japanese attack was driven off. The 2/10th, by now demoralized, was withdrawn. By the early hours of 29 August, the Japanese were at Rabi, their intended landing point on 25 August. There they outflanked a company of 25th Battalion, which, as had companies of 2/10th and 61st earlier in similar circumstances, took to the jungle north of the coastal track and succeeded in returning to friendly lines. At Kilarbo, the Japanese overran the bogged Australian anti-tank guns, but by now there were no tanks with the Japanese advance, as they too had succumbed to the flooded track and been abandoned near Rabi.

Most nights during the battle of Milne Bay, IJN cruisers and destroyers entered the bay, bombarding Allied positions. On the night of 29 August, they also brought reinforcements, 568 troops of *3rd Kure* and 200 of *5th Yokohama SNLF*, under Commander Yano Minoru, who took control of the whole force.

The next line to be defended by the Australians was the incomplete No 3 Strip, which provided a natural field of fire, with open ground 200 yards wide and almost a mile and a half long across the Japanese line of advance. The 61st Battalion held the left, extending to high ground, Stephen's Ridge, beyond the north-west end of the strip. The 25th Battalion was on the right. Both had 3in mortars. Here, United States units were first engaged in ground combat in Papua.

The 709th Anti-Aircraft Battery's .50cal machine guns were placed at either end of the line and 43rd Engineer Regiment's (ER) .30 and .50cal machine guns, mounted on half-tracks, were brought forward. Within comfortable range to the rear was a six-gun battery of 25-pdrs from 2/5th Field Regiment.

The reinforced Japanese attacked No 3 Strip at 0300hrs on 31 August. The force was 1,240 strong, not much more than the number of the defenders. The attack was poorly organized; not all companies were in position when it commenced.

No 3 Strip at Milne Bay. At 0300hrs on 31 August, the *SNLF* attacked across the strip from left to right. On the left side at the near end of the strip is Stephen's Ridge, where *No 5 Yokosuka SNLF* tried to outflank the Australian/American defence. At the top of the first bay (left) is Rabi, where the Japanese had intended to land. The second bay is Sanderson Bay. The Japanese landing point is beyond that. (Bradley Collection)

*Nos 3* and *5 Kure SNLF* attacked across the strip while *No 5 Yokosuka* attempted to turn 61st Battalion's left flank. The attack across the strip was hit by Australian artillery before it began, then shot down by a fusillade of fire thickened by American machine guns. It stalled quickly with heavy casualties. The flanking effort found 61st Battalion on Stephen's Ridge, but it also failed. The Japanese, who retreated before dawn, took 364 casualties, half of them dead. The Allied loss was three killed and 15 wounded. The two Japanese 37mm guns present were quickly knocked out by mortar fire. The rest of their artillery had not made it this far forward.

Soon after daylight on 31 August, with the repulse of what he judged to be the enemy's main effort, Clowes went on the offensive. The 2/12th Battalion was put in, advancing 3 miles east through knee-deep mud. Half the battalion halted at Gama River, the other half proceeded to KB Mission, which it took from a Japanese rearguard. That night at Gama River, the retreating *No 5 Yokosuka*, about 200 men, blundered into the rear half of 2/12th (with an element of 9th Battalion) and was driven off. At Gama River and KB Mission, Japanese casualties were close to 162, against 33 Australians killed and wounded.

Intelligence from MacArthur's headquarters mistakenly warned of another landing that night, causing Clowes to cancel his order to 2/9th to advance and take over the pursuit from 2/12th. No landing occurred and two companies of 2/12th advanced to Wadu Wadu Creek on 2 September, while 2/9th took luggers across the bay from Gili Gili wharf to KB Mission. That night, two Japanese cruisers, *Arashi* and *Hamakaze*, entered the bay once more, shelling Australian positions.

The following day, 2/12th advanced again, encountering a strong Japanese rearguard just west of Sanderson Bay. Even with artillery support, which wounded the Japanese commander Yano, the position could not be taken. The 2/9th passed through and continued the attack, but also failed. By the time a flanking move was organized, the Japanese had retired. The cost to both sides was around 60 casualties each. That evening, Japanese ships brought food and ammunition and took out wounded. Admiral Mikawa Gunichi decided to evacuate, so no more reinforcements landed.

On 4 September, 2/9th continued its advance. The battalion found the Japanese dug in south-east of Sanderson Bay along Whitton River, a mud-filled stream in a gully 3 miles west of the Japanese landing site. It was the last place the *SNLF* would offer determined organized resistance, as it was to cover the evacuation of the force. Here there was enough width in the flat coastal strip to add a flanking move to the formula. A 2/9th company lost its way, finding the Japanese landing site instead of getting behind the Whitton River defences. The company commander decided not to attack (for which he was relieved of command) and returned the way he had come.

The Australian attack at Whitton River was repulsed, costing 2/9th Battalion 23 dead and 34 wounded. The Japanese lost 60 killed and wounded. The next day, the Australian advance to Wahahuba found the Japanese gone. On the previous night, 5/6 September, the Japanese had evacuated 1,318 men of the 2,021 who had landed. The rest had been killed, were wounded and killed themselves, or were left behind to be killed or captured later in the month.

That night Japanese ships again entered the bay, looking for *SNLF* who had missed the evacuation. Finding the Australian supply ship *Anshun* at Gili Gili wharf, they sank it. The illuminated hospital ship *Manunda* was unmolested.

The evacuation marked the first time in World War II that a Japanese amphibious operation had landed, been defeated and the invasion force re-embarked. As MacArthur announced, the prime reason for Allied victory was 'complete surprise obtained by our preliminary concentration of superior forces'. The Australians had twice the infantry the Japanese had, as well as superior numbers of artillery, mortars and machine guns. They had close air support from No 1 Strip, while the Japanese air effort was ineffective. Vice Admiral Ugaki Matome added another reason for failure. The *SNLF* at Milne Bay, in his view, 'had inferior fighting spirit'.

Fourteen Americans were killed and six wounded. Of the Australians, 167 died and 203 were wounded. About 703 Japanese died at the battle of Milne Bay or, having missed the evacuation, were killed later. At least 321 were wounded.

An addendum to Milne Bay began on 22 October when 2/12th Battalion landed on Goodenough Island to kill or capture *5th Sasebo*, stranded there since 26 August. Some 71 had already been rescued by submarine, but 285 remained. The battalion at first could not find the Japanese, then failed to take their position over three days. When 2/12th attacked again on 25 October, *5th Sasebo* was no longer there, having been evacuated by barges sent down from Buna.

### *First Eora–Templeton's*

On the Kokoda Trail, weakened by Isurava, *144th Regiment* rested while *2/41st*, with a company of *3/41st* and other regimental elements, in total 1,305 men with four guns and an engineer company, pursued the Australians. The rearguard of the Australian force retreating from Isurava was composed of 2/16th and 2/14th Battalions, 710 men with one 3in mortar. Their task was to delay the Japanese advance until another stand could be made.

First Eora was the last time in the campaign when the Australians were significantly outnumbered and, at close to 2:1, it was the largest ratio by which the Japanese outnumbered the Allies in any fighting in Papua.

The rest of Maroubra Force fell back farther south, 39th Battalion to be rested in Port Moresby. The 53rd Battalion, owing to its poor performance at Isurava, was broken up, part of the battalion reforming as 55/53rd Battalion, to fight at Buna–Gona in December.

At dawn on 1 September, the Australian rearguard was 3 miles south of Isurava. It deployed on the heights south of and overlooking Eora Creek crossing, where the Trail crosses to the east side of the gorge. The stronger battalion, 2/16th, held the line while 2/14th was placed behind to deal with an enemy flanking move. Colonel Yazawa Kiyomi, in his first fight in Papua, decided to slip his main infantry unit, *2/41st* less one company, wide around the Australian left to cut the Trail in their rear, while pinning those in front with two companies. For a second time, *2/41st* wandered lost in the jungle at night looking for but not finding any Australians.

D Company, 39th Battalion on the Kokoda Trail. (Australian War Memorial 013288)

Yazawa's artillery and machine gun company set up on the same heights north-west of the creek crossing that the *Nankai Shitai* were to use for the same purpose in the fighting here in October during the Australian advance. They fired on 2/16th, which could be seen digging in on the opposite heights. When the lost battalion returned, Yazawa ordered it to attack the Australians directly. The *2/41st* was to fix the enemy front with one company, while two companies would feel their way around the Australian right, without going far from the Trail.

Before dawn on 2 September, the Japanese broke into the Australian position at the same time as the commander of the rearguard, Lieutenant Colonel Albert Caro, decided on a withdrawal. The fighting at the end was close, the Australian withdrawal was executed under considerable pressure and some wounded were not able to get away. Here, as elsewhere during the campaign, none who fell into Japanese hands survived. The loss to *41st Regiment* was 18 killed and 37 wounded. The Australians lost 17 killed and 12 wounded.

Contact was broken before first light on 2 September as 2/16th withdrew through 2/14th. The 2/16th halted half a mile south, short of Templeton's Crossing, then 2/14th fell back through them. By the evening of 2 September, the Australian rearguard was placed as it had been the previous evening, with 2/16th in front and 2/14th behind. The Japanese were not aware of the Australian retreat until they advanced on the morning of 2 September. Koiwai, the battalion commander, proceeded carefully, expecting the Australians had not gone far. Yazawa rebuked him for doing so. Before dark, Koiwai's scouts found the Australians again. To avoid what had happened in the last contact, when both flanks were threatened, Caro immediately withdrew. Following the Trail, they crossed back to the west side of Eora Creek and took up a position at the north end of Bamboo Ridge, where they were again attacked on the night of 3/4 September.

Yazawa repeated his pinning while flanking tactic. The flank attack penetrated 2/16th as far as battalion headquarters. Caro reported to Potts that his left had been driven in and the position could not be held. Caro's withdrawal was completed before dawn, ending the First Eora–Templeton's engagement, for the Australians a successful five-day rearguard action. Japanese casualties from 1 September to 5 September were 43 killed and 58 wounded. The Australians lost 21 killed and 54 wounded.

On 5 September, Horii, highly dissatisfied with Yazawa's speed of advance, barely more than a mile a day, ordered a two-battalion group of Kusunose's *144th Regiment* to take over the pursuit. Progress increased rapidly; Kusunose covered 25 miles in the next eight days.

### *Efogi/Brigade Hill*

During First Eora, the Australians abandoned their source of air-dropped supply, a dry lake at Myola, and fell back to Efogi. Potts, convinced he was heavily outnumbered, did not want to stop and fight, but Rowell told him to 'yield no more ground and regain initiative at earliest possible moment'. Potts selected a good position. Mission Ridge and Brigade Hill form one high boomerang-shaped feature offering excellent observation in the direction of the Japanese approach where there were, unusually, large patches of open ground affording opportunities for the air strikes Potts requested. There was rough terrain on both flanks. That on the Australian right was so difficult that Kusunose decided not to go that way. It was instead on the Australian left, along the low ground beside the Fagume River, where Kusunose chose to make his move.

Kusunose had his Regimental Headquarters (RHQ) including the RGC and two infantry battalions, each with their battalion gun platoon and a platoon of *15 IER*. The strength of *3/144th* was 589 and that of *2/144th* was 650. Adding regimental units and engineers to this, about 1,570 Japanese fought at Efogi. The important addition to Maroubra Force in early September was 2/27th Battalion, with 588 fresh men. The PIB was withdrawn. With the weak 2/14th and 2/16th and various minor detachments, there were 1,505 Australians and 10 RPC at Efogi.

Kusunose divided his command into three parts, an artillery and machine gun group, and his two infantry battalions. His plan was to pin the Australian front with one battalion while another executed a flanking move westward, around the Australian left. The artillery was located to support both attacks, on a bamboo grove on a knoll, a mile from 2/27th Battalion on Mission Ridge and almost 2 miles from 2/14th and 2/16th, which Potts had placed there to respond to a flank move. The bend in the Mission Ridge–Brigade Hill feature permitted the Japanese guns placed on the knoll to fire both on 2/27th in the forward position of Mission Ridge, and farther away on Brigade Hill. At the bamboo grove were massed the RGC of *144th Regiment* and the battalion guns of *2/144th* and *3/144th*, a total of two 75mm guns, two 70mm guns and two 37mm guns. The medium machine gun company of *3/144th*, equipped with telescopic sights, was placed forward of the artillery, 1,000 yards from 2/27th Battalion.

On 6 and 7 September, Allied aircraft, B-26 Marauders from 22nd Bombardment Group, bombed the Japanese assembling at Kagi. The first attack killed two and wounded two. When the second attack came, *144th* was caught in the open. Eight Marauders and four P-40s bombed and strafed the regiment, scattering the men and delaying the attack for several hours. Eleven were killed and 20 wounded. This was unusually good work. A week earlier, the same squadron had accidentally bombed 39th Battalion, hitting no one.

When the Japanese attack got under way on 7 September, two companies closed with Mission Ridge, with the task of drawing forward reserves. Potts did not take the bait. Japanese artillery alternatively supported *3/144th* on Mission Ridge and fired upon Brigade Hill where *2/144th*, about to execute its night flanking move, was expected to arrive next morning. On 8 September, *3/144th* withdrew a little while a deluge of heavy machine gun and mountain gun fire fell on 2/27th. The Japanese infantry's withdrawal to avoid the shooting of their own artillery allowed the Australian battalion to retire without the Japanese being aware of it. In the late afternoon, *3/144th* advanced, and in another instance common to jungle fighting, found their enemy gone. Early in the evening, with little contact with the Australians, they linked up with *2/144th* on Brigade Hill.

The events which brought about the withdrawal of 2/27th began with the movement of *2/144th* to the Australian rear on Brigade Hill. The previous day, a distinctive tree on the hill was pointed out to Major Horie, *2/144th*'s commander. Kusunose ordered Horie to place his battalion near the tree. Led by local Papuan guides, the battalion marched along the Fagume River, to just east of Enivilogo village, then turned directly uphill, in part following a track. They arrived on top of Brigade Hill at dawn without contact with the Australians. The Japanese flanking movement was much deeper than Potts anticipated, cutting him off from all three of his battalions.

It was soon apparent to the Australians immediately on either side of *2/144th* (MFHQ to the south and 2/16th, 2/14th and 2/27th Battalions to the north), that the Kokoda Trail was cut and Potts was separated from his command. His headquarters was fired on, the telephone line to the battalions was cut and wireless communication was intermittent. Artillery observers with the Japanese battalion began directing fire on Australian positions, which could now easily be seen.

Potts ordered a counter-attack from the north. Three hundred men, drawn from four companies of 2/14th and 2/16th Battalions, formed across the ridge on a front of around 100 yards, and assaulted south towards *2/144th*. Though a few dozen Australians cut their way through to Potts, the attack as a whole was a failure, costing 100 casualties. A later smaller attack in the other direction was made from MFHQ with the assistance of two platoons of 2/16th, the headquarters guard. This also failed and Potts decided to retreat. Those with him followed the Trail directly to Menari. Potts had told Caro, on the other side of *2/144th*, that if counter-attacks failed he should take command and cut his way out. Two battalions, 2/14th and 2/16th, headed east that night,

Papuans carrying wounded on the Kokoda Trail. (History and Art Collection/Alamy Stock Photo)

## BRIGADE HILL, 8 SEPTEMBER 1942 (PP. 46–47)

On 8 September 1942, the second day of the battle of Efogi/Brigade Hill, the Australian force was cut off by a Japanese battalion blocking the Kokoda Trail in their rear **(1)**. A counter-attack was ordered by Brigadier Potts. Elements of 2/16th Battalion attacked south-west along the slope of Brigade Hill on its east side, while elements of 2/14th Battalion (not shown) attacked on the western slope.

While attack as a whole failed, the bulk of C Company of 2/16th, on the Australian left **(2)**, cut its way through to MFHQ in the Australian rear. Few of 2/14th got through.

*No 5 Company* of *2/144th* **(3)** defended the eastern side of Brigade Hill, where C Company made its successful attack. The Japanese unit had been there since the night before and had dug in. The 127 men in the company were overrun during the Australian attack, losing lost 43 dead and 40 wounded.

A member of *No 5 Company*, Corporal Nishimura Kokichi **(4)**, was dug in just off the crest on the eastern side of hill. He was wounded by an Australian with a Thompson gun, taking three rounds in the shoulder. He survived the war, returning to Papua to find and inter Japanese dead from Brigade Hill and other battlefields. The scene here is informed by the author's interview with Nishimura.

From a knoll 100 yards to the rear of *No 5 Company*, the *2/144th Battalion's machine* gun company fired in support of the defenders **(5)**. The Japanese machine gunners were unable to see the left flank of the Australian attack (C Company, 2/16th Battalion in foreground), but fired effectively on the 2/14th Battalion on the right flank of the Australian attack on the far side of the ridge. This machine gun fire largely explains the failure of the 2/14th attack.

then turned south and got to Menari before the Japanese. The third cut-off battalion, 2/27th, departed last and was forced to detour farther east. The battalion marched through the jungle for two weeks, with little food, before it was able to find friendly faces.

Three Australian 3in mortars, with 105 rounds, had been airdropped at Myola and carried to Brigade Hill. For the first time, the Australians were able to respond effectively to Japanese long-range weapons, killing three and wounding 14 Japanese gunners. Total Japanese losses at Efogi, excluding the air attacks of 6 and 7 September, were 60 dead and 98 wounded. Eighty-seven Australians were killed and 77 wounded.

In light of *2/144th*'s heavy casualties, *3/144th* was directed to take up the pursuit. The Australian retreat continued though Menari and Nauro to Ioribaiwa, where the next stand was made.

Kusunose, the most effective Japanese commander to serve in Papua, achieved at Efogi what Horii and Yazawa had thrice failed to do, to pin the enemy to the front and, by placing a battalion around the flank into their rear, disperse their force. With a strength about equal to that of the dug-in Australians, Kusunose forced them out of a good position and inflicted as many casualties as he lost. The Japanese artillery was a major contributor to this achievement. In addition, Kusunose soon realized he had cut from their line of communication a large number of defenders, 2/27th Battalion. The battalion took no further part in the fighting in Papua until it was committed to the battle of Buna–Gona in November 1942. In effect, the Japanese success at Efogi removed, through casualties and the absent 2/27th Battalion, 700 Australians from their order of battle – half the Australian force. Japanese diaries and official reports stated that they believed they had broken the Australian 'fighting spirit'. Potts' deployment at Efogi was criticized, especially the large gap he had left on Brigade Hill between his infantry battalions and his headquarters. He was relieved of command.

## *Ioribaiwa*

On 10 September 1942, Brigadier Selwyn Porter replaced Potts as commander of Maroubra Force. The Australian force defeated at Efogi (less 2/27th) retreated to join Porter at Ioribaiwa where they were joined by the newly arrived 25th Brigade. Something more than another defensive stand was planned. While Porter's force held the Kokoda Trail, 25th Brigade was to leave the Trail south of Ioribaiwa and outflank the Japanese on both sides.

Brigadier Ken Eather's fresh AIF 25th Brigade had 1,861 men in three battalions. Under Porter, who by mutual agreement ceded command of Maroubra Force to Eather, there was also MFHQ, a composite battalion of 2/14th and 2/16th, a composite company from 21st Brigade, and 3rd Militia Battalion. With the usual minor units there were 2,957 Australians assembled. This was the largest concentration for battle so far achieved on the Kokoda Trail by the Australians. It was only possible to supply such a large force, at this early stage of the campaign when transport aircraft were few, because the Australians were now just 6 miles from their roadhead at Ower's Corner and 30 miles from Port Moresby.

Kusunose's pursuit group was essentially the force that fought at Efogi, less casualties and plus mountain artillery and medical personnel. Now with nine guns and 12 heavy machine guns Kusunose had close to 1,650 men. Australian firepower was less impressive. They had three Vickers medium machine guns, used for the first time on the Kokoda Trail, and three 3in mortars. However, 25th Brigade brought double the usual complement of Thompson submachine guns, giving two per section, a powerful addition for the close-range fighting that typified the campaign.

Eather's move to go around both Japanese flanks had barely begun when Kusunose's pursuit group arrived on 12 September. While Kusunose waited for his guns to come up, he probed the Australian position. It was to be his last battle in Papua. He was so ill that he ran the fight from his bed, and he was evacuated later in the campaign. Kusunose sent spotters out to locate targets for the artillery, which massed in one body on a slope north of Ioribaiwa Ridge. The next day, he sent *2/144th* off to the west to, as it had done twice before, swing around the Australian flank into their rear. *3/144th* would pin the enemy to the front. It was the Efogi plan again, but this time the appearance of Australian reinforcements was to thwart it.

Eather's attempt to envelop both Japanese flanks, a battalion on each side, with one in reserve, went slowly, as did all movement off tracks through the jungle. Lieutenant Colonel Alfred Buttrose, commanding the 2/33rd on the right, found the terrain impossible, prompting Eather to revise his plan. Buttrose brought his battalion back to the Trail then up to Ioribaiwa Ridge. From there it was to make a shorter right hook into Nauro in the Japanese rear, though this did not get going before Kusunose intervened. As 2/33rd arrived on the right of 3rd Battalion on 13 September, the composite battalion in the centre was attacked by the Japanese. Eather responded cautiously, holding 2/33rd in place to see how his 2/31st advance on his left progressed. Eather now had four battalions (counting the composite battalion as one) virtually in line abreast along the ridge, over a mile long, and one battalion in reserve.

While moving west along the narrow Ioribaiwa Ridge crest before turning north, the left prong of Eather's advance, 2/31st Battalion, collided head on with *2/144th* coming the other way along the ridge on 14 September. Both battalions threw a company out to each of their steeped-sloped flanks and butted against each other in the afternoon, to no effect. Meanwhile, against the Australian centre, one and a half Japanese companies of *3/144th*, plus elements of engineers, advanced against the composite battalion. Japanese guns fired in support while the battalion gun of *3/144th* was brought up to within 100 yards of the Australian trenches.

Throughout the Ioribaiwa action, Japanese artillery concentrated on the composite battalion. It inflicted a considerable number of casualties, causing the battalion to give ground. Kusunose, aware additional Australian battalions had arrived, still held half of *3/144th* in reserve and decided to use it in a new attack around his left (east). The flanking force surprised a company of 3rd Battalion which retreated, enabling the Japanese to insert themselves between the 3rd and 2/33rd Battalions. The Australian reserve, 2/25th Battalion, sent two companies to eject them, while 2/33rd sent one company to do the same from the other side of the Japanese insertion. The counter-attack failed because 2/33rd got lost.

In the Australian centre, it was the same story as the day before. At 0400hrs on 15 September, the Japanese attacked with a reinforced company of *3/144th*. They advanced on the Australian composite battalion while calling in an artillery bombardment. The *3/144th* gun was now brought to within 50 yards of the Australians. Firing rapidly, it inflicted heavy casualties on the composite battalion.

On 15 September, on the Australian left, 2/31st and *2/144th* continued to spar tentatively with one another. By evening, Kusunose had committed all his infantry and in two days of fighting had failed to drive the Australians off Ioribaiwa Ridge. If the Australians essayed a major counter-attack with their reserve, he had nothing spare with which to meet it.

On the morning of 16 September, the company of *3/144th*, on the Japanese left, enlarged its position by seizing what the Japanese called 'Sankaku Yama', a striking pyramid-shaped hill on the crest of Ioribaiwa Ridge. This was potentially serious as Sankaku Yama overlooked the spine of the ridge and it would be possible to enfilade the Australian line along the ridgetop with machine guns placed on the hill. The Japanese at Sankaku Yama stood off an attack by two companies of 2/33rd Battalion. With the failure of this effort, Eather contacted his divisional commander Allen, in Port Moresby, and obtained permission to withdraw. By evening, Maroubra Force was deployed on the next ridge to the south, Imita Ridge. The Japanese, outnumbered and fought to a standstill with no reserve in hand, were not in a position to interfere with the Australian retreat.

Australian casualties were 49 dead and 121 wounded from 13 to 17 September. It is probable that half the casualties were inflicted by Japanese artillery. Apart from infantry, there were few Japanese battle casualties. The massed Japanese artillery was not fired on by the Australian 3in mortars, or the Vickers machine guns, because it could not be located. Japanese casualties were 39 killed and about 120 wounded. Here, at the limit of the Japanese advance, their battle casualties thus far were 900 killed or wounded. Australian and Papuan casualties were slightly more, 464 killed and 567 wounded.

At Ioribaiwa, Kusunose had reached the position Horii intended: he was on the southern slope of the Owen Stanley Range, close enough to Port Moresby to threaten it and attack it when he was reinforced. His victory at Ioribaiwa was notable. He had been outnumbered almost 2:1 and was attacking a naturally strong position. While Kusunose's artillery gave him a decisive advantage, it had limited ammunition. He was too greatly outnumbered to drive off such a large Australian force, yet it had retreated. It has been said that it is not as important to defeat the enemy force so much as it is to convince their commander that he has lost the battle. It appears Eather believed he was defeated, so he was defeated.

## THE JAPANESE RETREAT

Eather took up a new position on Imita Ridge, one of the last suitable defensive positions before the rugged ridges all the way from Kokoda give way to less useful defensive terrain near Port Moresby. Here he had the support of artillery for the first time on the Kokoda Trail. Two 25-pdr guns from 14th Field Regiment were laboriously dragged forward to fire on Ioribaiwa Ridge.

With the Japanese within 20 miles of the outermost of General George Kenney's 5th Air Force air fields, Kenney became alarmed for his aircraft and his large dumps of bombs and fuel. He stated that if one Japanese crossed the Goldie River, 12 miles from Port Moresby, he would withdraw 5th Air Force to Queensland.

No Japanese did cross the Goldie River. Kusunose settled down on Ioribaiwa Ridge as Horii's orders limited how far he could advance; no attack was made on Imita Ridge. Hyakutake now told Horii to send *41st Regiment*, then in the mountains but well behind Kusunose, back to Buna. A week later, Horii was ordered to withdraw Kusunose's entire force. On 24 September, the Japanese retreated from Ioribaiwa. Events at Guadalcanal and Milne Bay were the catalyst of change. At Guadalcanal, Major General Kawaguchi Kiyotake's 13 September attack to take Henderson Field was badly defeated at Edson's Ridge. It would clearly be some time before troops could be spared for Papua. Also, Hyakutake's cryptanalysts advised that the Allies were about to advance from Milne Bay along the north coast of Papua towards Buna, in which case its garrison had to be strengthened. Buna remained on the alert for the rest of September, though no attack came. Such a move was indeed being discussed in Brisbane, where MacArthur's headquarters now was, but the Allied attack on Buna was not to take place until November.

Kusunose's men made a clean break. On 28 September, when the Australians, with the arrival of a fresh brigade, commenced their advance, they found empty trenches on Ioribaiwa Ridge. The *Nankai Shitai* retreated rapidly and their pursuers, advancing cautiously under a new commander, Major General Arthur Allen, did not see it again for two weeks.

Horii reorganized the *Nankai Shitai* into three parts. On the north coast at Buna to protect against the expected Allied landing, he placed *1/41st* and *3/41st* together with about 1,000 *SNLF* of the original force. Between the Kokoda Trail and the north coast, to act as a reserve for both, to rest them in the better supplied lowlands, and to guard against enemy emerging from the Owen Stanley Range on other tracks, he placed *2/41st* and two battalions of the *144th*. The third part was the *Stanley Detachment*, mainly *2/144th*. Its task was to hold a position in the mountains 'until conditions again favoured the Emperor's cause', which really meant once victory had been achieved at Guadalcanal. The *Stanley Detachment* dug in 22 miles north of Ioribaiwa, just beyond Myola, the dry lake. While not as much a threat to Port Moresby as Ioribaiwa, the Allies were worried that at any time the *Stanley Detachment* might be reinforced and resume the advance. This forced the Allies to keep a large enough force at Port Moresby to guarantee it would not fall. The less than 1,000 men of the *Detachment* contributed to keeping many thousands defending Port Moresby, thus not available to be used elsewhere. MacArthur took note of this apparent threat and insisted the planned advance to Buna on the north coast, which the Japanese had got wind of, could not draw on the Port Moresby garrison and could not commence until all the US 32nd Division arrived there from Australia.

### Second Eora–Templeton's

The Australian attacks in October on three successive lines held by the *Stanley Detachment*, the Japanese reinforcement of the *Detachment* and the subsequent Japanese defeat is known as the Second Eora–Templeton's action.

The placing of the first line of the *Stanley Detachment* was determined by Myola, the best place along the Kokoda Trail for air-dropping supplies. There was little point in withdrawing far enough into the mountains to cause the Australians a supply headache if they solved it at one stroke by free use of

Myola. The first Japanese position was thus placed on Bamboo Ridge, a mile north-west of the northern tip of the dry lake. Once the Australian advance reached Myola, air drops began, but they were seriously interrupted by fire from Bamboo Ridge and Japanese patrols probing to the edge of the dry lake.

The *Stanley Detachment*, commanded by Horie of *2/144th*, was initially a little short of 700 strong, with three guns. The main body at Bamboo Ridge was seconded by 150 men covering an alternative approach, a track from Efogi to Kagi to a junction with the Kokoda Trail north of Bamboo Ridge at Templeton's Crossing. These two positions were intended to buy a few extra days' digging time for two more lines of defence under construction.

A C-47 air-dropping food and ammunition at Nauro village in October 1942, during the Australian advance on the Kokoda Trail. (Australian War Memorial 027019)

By October, the Australians had assembled a powerful force for their advance, with Buna as the objective. There were 4,600 Australians, in seven infantry and one pioneer battalion, and 2,100 Papuan carriers forward of the roadhead. However, in the first period of fighting when the two Japanese outer positions were attacked, half of this force, now called 7th Australian Division rather than Maroubra Force, was not engaged. The force in contact with the Japanese was part of Eather's 25th Brigade. Eather's divisional commander was Major General Arthur Allen, but Allen's superior was no longer Rowell. Blamey had flown to Port Moresby at MacArthur's insistence to 'energise the situation'. He did so by replacing Rowell, Commander, New Guinea Force, with Lieutenant General Edmund Herring on 28 September.

The four battalions of 25th Brigade had been depleted by battle casualties and sickness to 1,882 men. The 2/31st Battalion was held in reserve at Kagi. Two battalions, 2/33rd and 3rd, went to Bamboo Ridge and another, 2/25th, marched along the Kagi track. At the start of the engagement 1,400 Australians opposed 670 Japanese.

On 12 October, 2/25th Battalion advanced on the Kagi track with orders to take Templeton's Crossing. In three days' fighting, the battalion made no impression on the 150 Japanese it faced. On the morning of 15 October, the Japanese had disappeared and the battalion advanced to Templeton's Crossing.

On the main track, along the north–south aligned Bamboo Ridge, 2/33rd opposed 520 Japanese, each company behind the other, all in separate all-round defence. The attack commenced when 2/33rd, with a 3in mortar in support, put in three companies. Under fire from Japanese artillery, they failed to dent the line. The 3rd Battalion was brought up to swing around the Japanese right, while patrols tried to penetrate gaps between the Japanese companies. Aware the Australians were in strength and threatening to cut them from Templeton's, the *Stanley Detachment* retreated early in the morning of 15 October, the same moment that the Japanese in front of 2/25th withdrew. Casualties for the fighting on both tracks were 30 Japanese dead with the same number wounded, against 15 Australians killed and 49 wounded.

Tsukamoto, who commanded *1/144th*, replaced Horii as *Stanley Detachment* commander. The *Detachment* now occupied the second line of defences, the main position, 550 yards deep along the Kokoda Trail north of Templeton's Crossing. The third line, at Eora village, where the first Eora action had been fought early in September, was insurance against failure at Templeton's Crossing. The Templeton's position was well chosen; the Eora Creek crossing of the Kokoda Trail was overlooked by the defenders and the two battalion guns and one 37mm gun present could fire down along the line of the Australian approach from the south. A Japanese mountain gun was placed 1,000 yards north to fire down the gorge of Eora Creek, as it did at 2/33rd leading the advance. The one weakness of the Japanese Templeton's position was that it was itself overlooked from high ground running north along the Japanese left (east). An Australian attack coming from this high ground was to be the deciding movement in this second phase of the Eora–Templeton's fighting.

Templeton's was held by 800 Japanese. Allen ordered up the newly arrived 16th Brigade under Brigadier John Lloyd. Allen's plan was to use them to replace the worn 25th Brigade, but as each new battalion was fed into the fight, the one it was to replace was not always withdrawn. Seven battalions were now available – in itself testimony to the advantage conferred by the increase in the air-dropping of supplies at Myola, made possible when the Japanese lost Bamboo Ridge. There were 1,850 men in 16th Brigade and 1,520 in the four battalions of 25th Brigade. Fighting power was further enhanced by eight 3in mortars and four Vickers medium machine guns, though ammunition was limited. Now, as the Japanese had been doing to the Australians, the Australians could bombard with mortars, and lay down suppressing fire with machine guns as their infantry assaulted. While Australian supply was improved by Myola, that of the Japanese deteriorated. From 9 to 13 September, heavy rain washed away the Japanese supply line in the lowlands north of the mountains, including several lengths of the Sanananda road and 30 bridges large and small. As a result, the *Stanley Detachment*, 80 miles from Buna, began to starve. Later the Australians found that some dead Australian soldiers had been eaten.

During 17–20 October, five of Allen's seven battalions were involved in the fighting, giving the Australians, overall, a 4:1 superiority, more than enough to break the Japanese position. The 16th Brigade, under Brigadier John Lloyd, had 2/1st, 2/2nd and 2/3rd Battalions. They were the first battalions raised in the AIF in 1939, had the greatest experience of successful battle in the Middle East and the benefit of several months' jungle training in Ceylon while returning to Australia. They were the highest-quality Australian infantry encountered by the Japanese thus far. The 2/2nd Battalion, having worked its way around to the heights east of the Japanese, which was the flaw in the defenders' position, drove down from there on 20 October, cutting the Kokoda Trail in the middle of the Japanese defences. At the same time, 2/1st Battalion attacked north directly along the Trail, breaking into the Japanese trenches. Tsukamoto saw that the position, penetrated in two places, was lost. He ordered a withdrawal without consulting Horii. There was time to bring all Japanese guns out. This second phase of Eora–Templeton's cost the Japanese 36 dead and 35 wounded against the Australian loss of 54 dead and 68 wounded.

When Horii learned of the sudden collapse at Templeton's, he used the reserve he had assembled in the lowlands on the Sanananda road.

He ordered everyone he could lay his hands on to march to the Eora village position, the third line he had not expected to need. Some 495 men were fed into the battle as they arrived between 22 and 27 October.

By 27 October, 1,050 Japanese were in the Eora Creek line. Against this, the Australians had the same seven battalions in two brigades. Lloyd had detachments from a field company, divisional and medical units; 1,770 infantry and about 2,100 men in all. This was thrice the number of the defenders as this phase of the fighting began and closer to twice the defenders' number as it ended.

Eora was a well-prepared position, in a way too well prepared, for it was designed for a force larger than the one available to defend it. Tsukamoto placed *2/144th* in the centre at Eora, covering the creek crossing. On its flanks were the other two battalions, *1/144th* holding the Japanese left and *3/144th* some distance behind *2/144th* to the Japanese right, holding the high ground where the Japanese artillery was – a 37mm gun, two battalion guns and one, later two, mountain guns. This high ground was the key to the position as artillery there could place direct fire on the possible Australian approaches. Unfortunately, to benefit from the advantages offered by the artillery position, hold the creek crossing and prevent the Australians gaining access to the Kokoda Trail by turning the Japanese left, there had to be a weakness somewhere. In the right centre, there was a thinly covered gap of 650 yards between *2/144th* and *3/144th*, which, owing to thick jungle there, the Australians failed to find. Jungle fighting is like night fighting in that visibility is usually 10–30 yards. In the Owen Stanley Range, the sun rarely penetrates far through the canopy of trees, the enemy are not often seen and patrols looking for gaps in defences cannot easily find one. If they do, without accurate maps, they cannot report exactly where they found an enemy weakness.

From 22 to 24 October, Lloyd's 16th Brigade, spurred on by Allen who was hearing threatening noises from Blamey to get moving, made a frontal assault on the Eora crossing position: Cullen's 2/1st Battalion crossed Eora Creek and penetrated a short way into the ground held by *2/144th*, but was stopped. Lloyd then brought 2/2nd to the right of 2/1st, where it encountered *1/144th*, and committed 2/3rd in an attack from the Australian left. This attack of 2/3rd Battalion on 28 October was the key move. It broke into the lines of *3/144th* on the high ground north-west of the creek crossing, where the Japanese artillery was. This attack went very well, because it caught the Japanese in the midst of abandoning the entire Eora line – the guns had already departed. Once again, events in Guadalcanal dictated those in Papua. The Japanese failed on land at Guadalcanal on the night of 24/25 October in the battle of Henderson Field. Consequently, Horii was ordered to withdraw the *Stanley Detachment* on 28 October. Horii was to pull all his force back 35 miles, abandoning Kokoda, out of the mountains down to the Sanananda road towards the Wairopi crossing of the Kumusi River.

From 22 to 29 October, the Australians lost 72 killed and 154 wounded. The Japanese lost 64 killed and 70 wounded. That half of the Japanese dead were lost on the last day of fighting, against seven Australian dead, indicates that, caught in the midst of a withdrawal, the Japanese suffered accordingly. That 43 Australians were killed in the first frontal attack period, 22–24 October, against 23 Japanese, also says something about the lack of success in this phase of the Australian attack. Battle casualties for all three phases of

Second Eora were 412 Australians and 244 Japanese. Strategically, Second Eora was important as the Australians could now exit the Owen Stanley Range and the Kokoda airstrip would soon be in their hands.

The day following the victory, Allen was sacked as 7th Division commander. Allen's superiors thought he had been too slow and cautious, even before he contacted the Japanese. Since 28 September, he had advanced only 35 miles in a month. Outnumbering the Japanese by 3:1, sometimes 4:1, he had taken 16 days to carve his way through the three *Stanley Detachment* lines of defence. Allen's view was he did not want to wear down his force by going quickly, he expected a Japanese counter-attack, and he wanted a large reserve of supplies built up before each advance. On 26 October, Blamey signalled to MacArthur 'since 21 October progress has been negligible against an opponent much fewer in number'. This was, replied MacArthur, 'NOT repeat NOT satisfactory.' Allen, having won the battle, was relieved of command. If there was a chance to get to Buna via Kokoda before the Japanese could reinforce it, then Allen's superiors were prepared to take risks. In such a circumstance, a subordinate running the battle who is unwilling to take those risks was seen to be a liability.

## PREPARATIONS FOR AN ALLIED THRUST

In September, the Japanese intelligence cell in Rabaul became aware there was to be a second Allied offensive in Papua, apart from that on the Kokoda Trail, and that it would be directed at Buna. They were right that one was planned, but wrong about when and where. They believed there would be a direct amphibious assault on Buna beaches in September. In fact, Buna would not be attacked until November and there would not be an amphibious landing. Rather there would be an air and sea move of 32nd Division to the north coast of Papua, not far south of Buna, and a landward advance from there.

It would take some time to move troops forward by air over the mountains and by coastal luggers via Milne Bay, which now had three strips in operation and improved wharf facilities. Most of the men and the equipment had to come from the east coast of Australia. Port Moresby harbour, which once had the capacity to handle only 500 tons of cargo per day, was increased to eight times that, Milne Bay to four times its earlier capacity. Two regimental combat teams of the US 32nd Division were sent to Port Moresby, completing the move by 28 September. Engineers, with protecting infantry, were advanced to small north coast airstrips, which were constructed or upgraded at Fasari, Wanigela and Pongani, 20–60 miles south-east of Buna. The first step was taken on 5 October, a week before Second Eora commenced, when 2/10th Battalion and a US anti-aircraft battery was flown into Wanigela from Milne Bay.

Transport by air, which was to be stretched to the limit, would bring in most

*SNLF* infantry doing mortar drill with Type 97 81mm mortar at Buna. (Public domain via Wikimedia Commons)

of the troops. Supplies would mainly come by sea from Milne Bay. The idea of marching men over the mountains on a more easterly route than the Kokoda Trail was abandoned after the experience of the Americans of 2nd Battalion, 126th Regiment, who took five weeks to get to Buna and arrived in an exhausted and malnourished state.

The option to attack Buna along the north coast of Papua was made possible by an increase in resources. The US Small Ships Section gathered and administered coastal craft, luggers, captured Japanese Daihatsu barges and schooners with too shallow a draft to be bothered by the coral reefs at Cape Nelson on the Milne Bay to Buna sea route. The air move was made possible by a tripling of transport aircraft to almost 60 and capable of lifting more than a battalion a day. Each Douglas C-47 could carry 28 men or two and a half tons of cargo. The US 32nd Division slowly assembled in the areas of Abel's Field, Wanigela, Natunga and Pongani. Then by a combination of marching and hopping along the coast in small craft, they would attack Buna from the south-east.

Over the next five weeks, from 5 October, a force of 7,000, mainly US 32nd Division, flew to the assembly area. Engineers remained to improve facilities while the infantry headed north. By mid-November, over 6,000 were assembled in the Bofu, Natunga, Oro Bay, Pongani rectangle, 10–20 miles south of Buna. This second Allied offensive was, at first, to be a cautious one; plans were made to extract the force should the worst happen. MacArthur and Blamey were mindful of the possibility that Guadalcanal might fall to the Japanese, in which case thousands of Japanese reinforcements could be expected to arrive at Buna, or Milne Bay, or there might even be another attempt on Port Moresby by sea. The risk they were prepared to run on the Kokoda Trail–Sanananda road route – which resulted in the sacking of Allen – was one they were not prepared to run on the north coast where, should the Japanese react strongly in the air, the supply line would collapse and 32nd Division be cut off.

Now and again, the *SNLF* from the Buna garrison sent patrols by sea along the north coast as far as 120 miles south-east, over half way to Milne Bay. Incredibly, they did not detect the Allied build-up.

## *Oivi–Gorari*

In October, Hyakutake, with *17th Army* Headquarters, moved from Rabaul to Guadalcanal where he would attempt to run both the campaign there and the one in Papua. Hyakutake left on 9 October but Colonel Miyazaki Chuichi, his chief of staff, did not leave until 29 October. Miyazaki told Horii that, after the defeat at Second Eora, Horii should halt his retreat west of the Kumusi River where there was a huge supply dump. The reluctance to abandon food and ammunition accumulated there – the dump was so large it could not possibly be moved within a reasonable time – played a part in determining where the Japanese would next make a stand. In order to cover the supply dump, it was necessary to hold a position well forward of it; Oivi Heights was the obvious choice. To hold a bridgehead after a retreat – the Oivi–Gorari position can be considered a bridgehead west of the Kumusi River – also signals intent to renew the offensive at some future point, or at the very least a determination to retain the option to do so. At the beginning of November, the basic Japanese plan had not changed: throw everything at Guadalcanal, solve that problem then reinforce

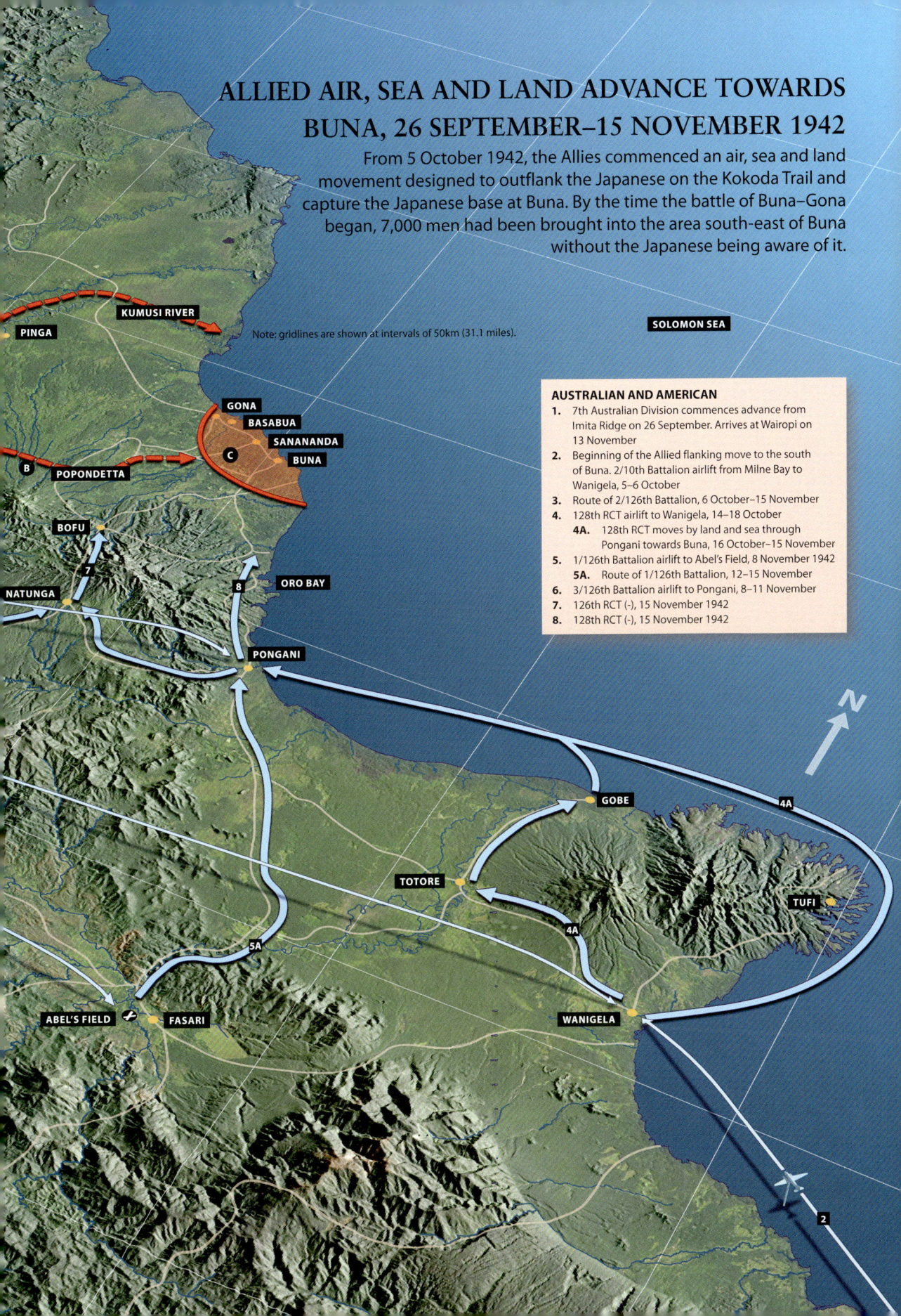

Papua and attack Port Moresby. The difference now was the starting point would be the Kumusi bridgehead.

At Oivi, steep slopes with suitable artillery positions faced west towards Kokoda. The Ajule Kajale Range runs parallel to the Sanananda road to the north and Hydrographers Range runs parallel to the south. The Oivi Heights is a link of high ground between the two. Another advantage was thick jungle on the high ground which concealed defenders, while thinner coverage on the low ground to the west in front of the heights aided Japanese observation of the Australians.

Oivi did have a weakness. The northern and southern ranges were too far apart and the whole distance could not be closely defended. There was a gap of lower ground on the southern side, with a track leading into the Japanese rear.

Within the defences, prepared in late October, Horii placed his freshest troops, Yazawa's *41st Regiment*, on the Oivi Heights. As the rearguard, *1/144th*, was placed west of Oivi and was to fall back through the Oivi defences, delaying the Australian advance from Kokoda. As it arrived within the Oivi line, *1/144th* came under Yazawa's command. Three miles east of Oivi was the main body of *144th Regiment*, in reserve at Gorari. It could march west and reinforce *41st Regiment*, or south-west to block the track that ran parallel to the main track and led to the Kumusi, the track the Australians later attacked along. *41st Regiment* had 1,377 men, *144th* had 891 and there were 15 guns. For the first time, a large engineer company of 200 men was deployed for battle. With other detachments, the *Nankai Shitai* had 2,800 men.

The Australian 7th Division, under Allen's replacement, Major General George Vasey, had orders to advance to the sea. At Alola, Vasey split his force. His 16th Brigade advanced by the most direct route, along a track across to the east side of Eora gorge, which passed south of Oivi (though two of its battalions were briefly drawn into the fight there). Simultaneously, 25th Brigade advanced on Kokoda. On 2 November, 2/31st patrols entered Kokoda unopposed. The two Australian axes of advance resulted in two separate but related combats. One was along the main route from Kokoda to Oivi, the Sanananda road, against *41st Regiment* on the Oivi Heights. The other occurred east of Oivi near Gorari, where *144th* was engaged.

25th Australian Infantry Brigade witness a flag-raising on the recapture of Kokoda, 2 November 1942. (Australian War Memorial 013572)

The 7th Division had seven infantry battalions. All had been in the mountains for one to two months and were reduced by one-quarter or one-third. Battalion strengths as Oivi–Gorari began were between 372 and 450, a total of 3,009 infantry against 1,800 Japanese infantry. Adding division staff and signals, brigade staffs, field ambulances and so forth, there were about 3,700 Australians present. Vasey was about to attack a strong position with neither artillery, nor a great superiority in numbers.

Against the 15 Japanese guns and 30 Juki heavy machine guns, the Australians now had ten Vickers heavy machine guns and ten 3in mortars, their capabilities much enhanced by the proximity of Kokoda strip. In the mountains, mortars rarely had more than 24 rounds each, but now, with ammunition supplied by air to Kokoda strip, only 5 miles in their rear, the Australians were able to deliver sustained mortar bombardments.

On 3 November, a Japanese rearguard west of Oivi withdrew after contact and the next day stood again briefly, then retired into the main Oivi defences. On 5 November, 2/3rd Battalion attacked Oivi Heights and was roughly handled. On 6 November, 2/2nd, 2/3rd and two companies of 3rd Battalion attacked, searching for the flanks. On the Japanese right, *2/41st* had all its four infantry companies in a line extending as far north as possible. Attacking where they believed the flank to be, the Australians instead hit the Japanese centre and were repulsed.

On the Japanese southern flank at Oivi, the Australians had more success. They threatened to get around the left of Major Miyamoto Saburo's *1/41st*. It was his battalion's first fight since arriving in Papua, as they had until now been a part of the Buna garrison. Unlike *2/41st*, he held one infantry company as a reserve. The company counter-attacked on 6 November, blocking the Australian threat to the southern flank of the Oivi line. The company was to have been supported by an attack by a company of engineers from *55 ER*. In a clear sign of deterioration in the *Nankai Shitai*, the company refused to advance. Fighting on the Australian right at Oivi continued on 7 November then settled down to a stalemate. As no headway could be made against Oivi, Vasey decided to throw his main weight against the Japanese rear at Gorari via the southern track. The Japanese at Oivi were kept engaged at minimum cost. The mortar bombardment continued and the 5th Air Force dropped eight tons of bombs, inflicting only a handful of casualties.

Meanwhile, Lieutenant Colonel Paul Cullen's 2/1st Battalion was on the track which ran parallel to the Kokoda–Sanananda road and south of it. His task was to find a way into the Japanese rear. Orokaiva scouts informed Horii that there were Australians on this track. Cullen moved east on 6 November, missing the track junction he was looking for. When he realized he was almost at the Kumusi River, he retraced his steps, finding the right track to Gorari.

As Cullen was going the wrong way on 6 November, Vasey made his decision. He believed there was enough promise in Cullen's advance and enough evidence, in the form of casualties without result, to show the Oivi approach was a dead end. He committed three more battalions along Cullen's route. Eather was to take the three battalions of 25th Brigade, follow up 2/1st and take that battalion under command. With four battalions, he was to cut the Sanananda road in the Japanese rear.

While Horii was negligent in leaving the southern track almost undefended, he responded promptly. He had most of *144th* in reserve for just such an eventuality and moved it to Baribe, two-thirds of the way from Gorari to Cullen's track junction. There, the regiment dug in blocking the Australian advance. Horii, aware that the Australian pressure on Oivi was easing off, also ordered *1/144th* to leave *41st Regiment* and head east to hold Gorari.

Thus on 8 November, when 2/31st led the advance of four Australian battalions towards Gorari, they encountered over 700 men of *144th Regiment* at Baribe, a few miles short of Gorari. Here the Australians acted with a boldness not seen so far in the campaign. Cutting through the jungle, 2/25th came out on a track behind the Japanese at Baribe, surrounding them with the help of 2/31st. The other two Australian battalions continued on towards Gorari. There on 9 November, 2/33rd Battalion attacked *1/144th* and drove it off, taking Gorari village. With 2/33rd was 2/1st, which turned east from Gorari and found Horii's *Nankai Shitai* Headquarters (NSHQ) and the company protecting it. Horii personally organized a counter-attack, which failed.

With the Australians now on the Sanananda road, communications between NSHQ and the several parts of the *Nankai Shitai* were cut. Horii did not know if the main body of *144th* at Baribe was still holding on, had been destroyed or had retreated to the Kumusi. At Oivi, Yazawa's *41st Regiment* had heard nothing from Horii since 8 November and he was unaware *1/144st* no longer held Gorari.

On 9 November, *17th Army*, out of touch with the disaster unfolding, decided Horii should abandon the supply dump and make a measured retreat across the Kumusi River, to be completed by 16 November. By the morning of 10 November, Horii realized there was not that much time available and an immediate retreat was ordered, lest the *Nankai Shitai* be destroyed. Having lost signals communications, Horii sent out runners to inform his subordinates. Something more resembling a rush to the rear than a retreat now took place.

The runner for Yazawa found him and *41st* pulled out of Oivi Heights unseen on the night of 10/11 November. The Australians found the Oivi Japanese trenches deserted the next morning. Cut off from their normal crossing place, *41st* marched east, then north along the west bank of the Kumusi. Abandoning all seven guns, they crossed the Kumusi at Pinga, well north of Wairopi on 14 November. The Australian 3rd Battalion was in pursuit and found Japanese dead, including wounded who had committed suicide. About 1,100 of the regiment reached the far side of the Kumusi, and almost all of these men arrived on the coast near Buna in time to participate in that battle.

The messenger from Horii to *144th* did not get through, but Tsukamoto had already decided on retreat. On the same night *41st* retired, Tsukamoto abandoned his six guns and cut his way through the Australians on the front of 2/25th Battalion, crossing the Kumusi just south of Wairopi. Fortunately for the Japanese, the Kumusi was low and no one was lost in the crossing. The *1/144th* also abandoned its two guns and escaped across the river. In the confusion, Horii was separated from his headquarters. He went downriver to find a crossing. Several days later at the mouth of the Kumusi, he and his batman found a canoe to paddle along the coast towards Buna. The canoe upset in rough water and Horii drowned. The batman survived to give an account of the end of the commander of the *Nankai Shitai*. In varying degrees of disarray, but with better fortune than attended Horii, the Japanese survivors of Oivi–Gorari made their way to Gona, Sanananda and Buna.

Weapons captured at Oivi–Gorari: the Type 92 gun, as used by battalion gun companies, and the Type 96 light machine gun, the standard section/squad weapon. (Australian War Memorial 013644)

Australian losses were 121 killed and 225 wounded. *144th Regiment* lost 196 dead and six men were captured. The other major unit, *41st Regiment*, did not lose heavily while at Oivi, but the *41st Regiment* company defending Horii's headquarters was surrounded and wiped out by 2/1st Battalion. The total number of Japanese dead was about 440. Many wounded could not get away and chose to stay to die, but 380 did escape.

At Oivi–Gorari in early November 1942, something had changed. Japanese generalship and fighting power were no longer what they had been, while those of the Australians had improved. The Japanese had lost a third of their force. Another marker of serious defeat is the loss of artillery pieces to the enemy. In no battle so far had this occurred to the Japanese, but at Oivi–Gorari, the *Nankai Shitai* lost every one of its 15 guns.

There were three factors that gave victory to the Australians. First, they held Kokoda. Having an airstrip just 5 miles west of Oivi increased many times over their ammunition supply. Second, the Australians were fitter and healthier than their enemy, the opposite of the situation in August and September. By Oivi–Gorari, there were signs the cumulative effect of over three months in a hostile climate on short rations was having a serious effect on the Japanese, while the Australians at Oivi–Gorari were not the same men who had fought through August and September. None present at Oivi–Gorari, except 3rd Battalion, had been forward of Port Moresby for more than two months, half had been there just a month. The daily sickness rate for the Japanese was approaching 100 while the Australian rate was now half that.

The third factor was generalship. The boldness of Vasey's move, in thrusting an entire brigade into the rear of a Japanese force, was comparable to the aggressive generalship of Kusunose. That it should work, against a force Vasey did not much outnumber, further supports the view that the quality of the *Nankai Shitai* had seriously deteriorated.

Since late July, the Australians had committed twice the number of troops the Japanese had to the Kokoda Trail fighting. The Japanese committed 4,700 men to the Trail, though 1,100 of them only fought in the last battle. This was not much more than a third of the total force that landed in Papua, but just over half of its fighting units. The rest never left Buna and some non-combat units had returned to Rabaul.

Oivi–Gorari was the conclusion of the Kokoda Trail phase of the campaign in which Japanese battle casualties were 2,050 against 1,760 Australians. The final act of the Papuan Campaign was played out at the battle of Buna–Gona, 30 miles to the north-east, beginning a few days later.

# THE BATTLE OF BUNA–GONA

On 16 November, the advance on Buna, Sanananda and Gona began. South of the Giruwa River, 6,200 Americans of 126th and 128th Regimental Combat Teams (RCT), which had been transported by air to landing strips at Pongani, Wanigela and Abel's Field, headed north on two tracks. The former via Dobodura on an inland route towards Buna village, the latter along the coast (together with 110 men from the 2/6th Australian Independent Company) to the same objective. North of the Giruwa River, two Australian brigades, victors of Oivi–Gorari, came from the Kumusi River in the west: 25th

32nd Division advancing on Buna, 15 November 1942. (Afro American Newspapers/Gado/Getty Images)

Unloading a 25-pdr artillery piece at Oro Bay, November 1942. The barge is a Japanese Daihatsu captured at Milne Bay in September. (Historic Collection/Alamy Stock Photo)

Brigade towards Gona, 16th Brigade to Sanananda. Vasey commanded the Australians, Major General Edwin Harding the Americans. Both were under Lieutenant General Herring, who arrived at Popondetta on 28 November, leaving Blamey to control events elsewhere in Papua and New Guinea.

The Australians, having fought for two months on the Kokoda Trail, were at two-thirds strength, with a total of 3,200 men in seven battalions. With them was one US infantry battalion, the 800-strong 2/126th, which had marched for five weeks over the Owen Stanley Range. It was sent across the Giruwa before fighting began and replaced by 3/126th. Some 10,200 Allied troops, in total, were closing in on Buna.

It was not until the day the advance began that the Japanese realized what was afoot. They knew of the Australian advance from the west, but had no knowledge of the weeks-long build-up of 32nd Division at airstrips to the south until Japanese air reconnaissance found troops unloading from barges at Hariko and Oro Bay, 5 and 15 miles south-east of Buna.

The Japanese responded. At dusk on 16 November, 14 fighters struck a convoy of four vessels, sinking all. General Harding was one of those forced to swim ashore. Two 25-pdr field guns were lost with 46 tons of food and ammunition, one week's worth for the entire American force. With no reserve supply, this was a disaster. Next morning, two more luggers were lost in the same way. The 32nd Division's already meagre supply line did not recover to the 16 November level for three weeks.

Allied estimates of the strength of the Buna garrison varied. Harding thought

# The battle of Buna–Gona, 15 November–9 December 1942

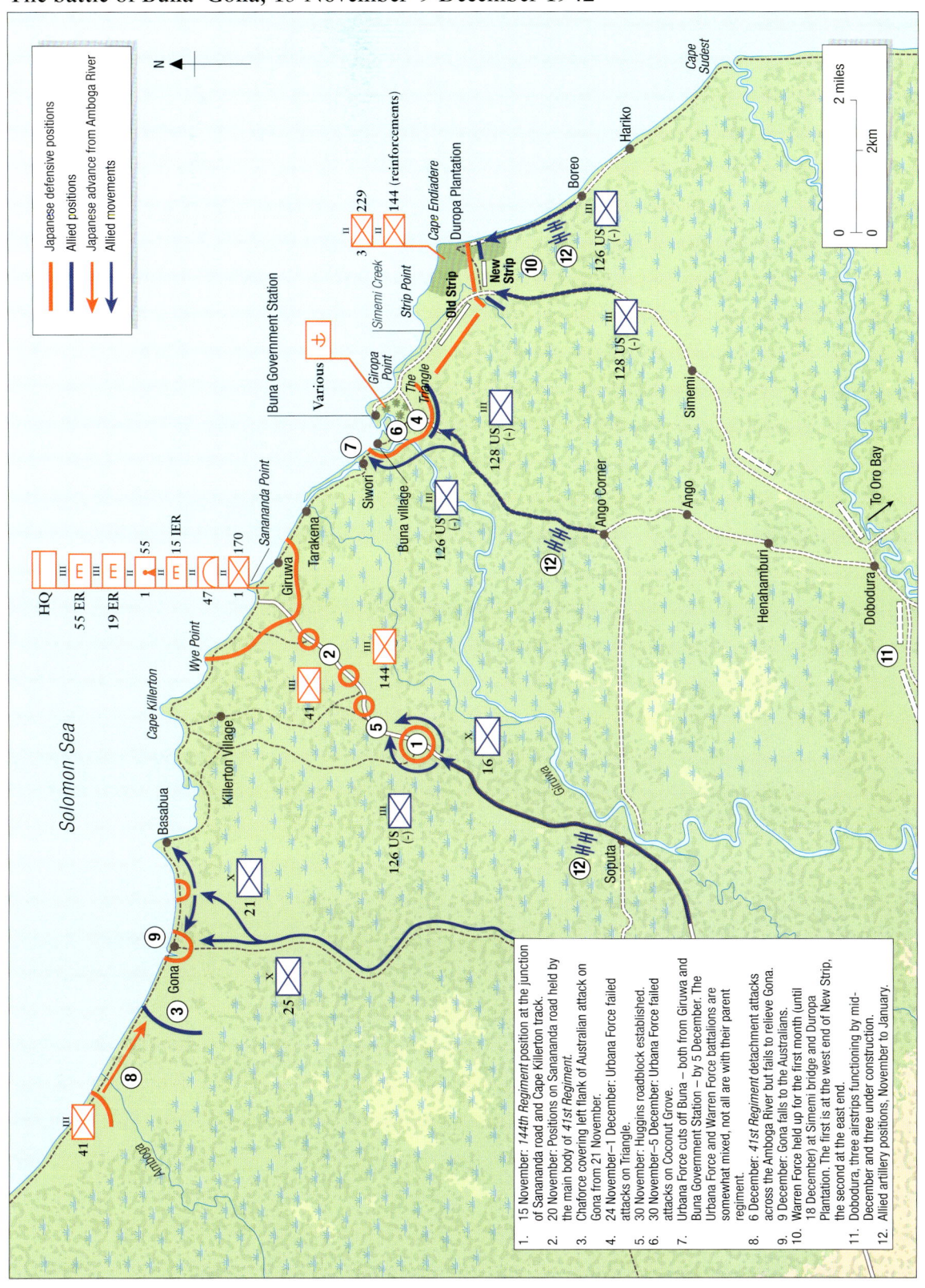

1. 15 November: *144th Regiment* position at the junction of Sanananda road and Cape Killerton track.
2. 20 November: Positions on Sanananda road held by the main body of *41st Regiment*.
3. Chaforce covering left flank of Australian attack on Gona from 21 November.
4. 24 November–1 December: Urbana Force failed attacks on Triangle.
5. 30 November: Huggins roadblock established.
6. 30 November–5 December: Urbana Force failed attacks on Coconut Grove.
7. Urbana Force cuts off Buna – both from Giruwa and Buna Government Station – by 5 December. The Urbana Force and Warren Force battalions are somewhat mixed, not all are with their parent regiment.
8. 6 December: *41st Regiment* detachment attacks across the Amboga River but fails to relieve Gona.
9. 9 December: Gona falls to the Australians.
10. Warren Force held up for the first month (until 18 December) at Simemi bridge and Duropa Plantation. The first is at the west end of New Strip, the second at the east end.
11. Dobodura, three airstrips functioning by mid-December and three under construction.
12. Allied artillery positions, November to January.

Air photograph of Japanese bunkers and trenches at Buna. Cape Endiadere is at the top right. (Public domain via Wikimedia Commons)

only a few hundred Japanese would be present because they were already evacuating. Vasey guessed there were 1,500 and Brigadier Charles Willougby, MacArthur's intelligence chief, thought there were 4,000, and they would stay and fight. None were aware of the Japanese defences. Begun in August, with work redoubled in October as the situation turned sour in the Owen Stanley Range, the Japanese fortification, the design of Colonel Yokoyama, was a masterpiece. Hundreds of bunkers, some of concrete and steel, studded four separate positions, stretching 11 miles along the coast in all, at Gona, Sanananda, along the road to Kokoda in front of Sanananda, and from Buna to Cape Endiadere. Most bunkers were built from coconut logs a foot thick. Owing to the high water table, they were half above ground, but well camouflaged by the quick-growing jungle. The bunkers were used for protection against air attack, artillery and mortar bombardment. They were impervious to anything but a direct hit from a 105mm howitzer, of which the Allies had only one. The 25-pdr field guns had too flat a trajectory to be as effective. After a bombardment, the Japanese would disperse from the bunkers via a network of trenches leading to numerous dug-in firing positions, ready to face the assault.

Three of the four fortified areas backed on to the sea and communication between them was good. The opposite was the case for the attackers, for the area was mainly swamp, often chest deep and sometimes over the height of a soldier. Allied approaches were limited to narrow lanes of slightly higher land, from 20 to a few hundred yards wide, which the local tracks naturally ran along, and where the strongest defences were placed. When it rained, as it did almost every day, or at high tide, even the tracks were submerged. The swamps either side of the tracks contained thick, tangled jungle growth.

A 32nd Division patrol, Buna, December 1942. (Bettmann via Getty Images)

The Allied advance might have started earlier, but was delayed by caution: if the Japanese won at Guadalcanal, thousands would be transferred to Buna. A second reason for delay was the need to build up enough supplies to support a few days' fighting. It was a costly delay as, a day before the Allies arrived, the Japanese received a large reinforcement, all of it going to the American front in the Buna–Cape Endiadere sector. Had the Americans come a day or two earlier, they would have found Buna the most thinly held sector; only 1,050 Japanese, *SNLF* and naval pioneers, holding the almost 3-mile-long Buna perimeter. However, an additional 1,450 Japanese arrived by sea on 18 and 19 November (including *3/229th*), and all were sent there, giving 2,500 defenders at Buna the day the battle began.

In the entire position, from Gona in the north-west to Buna in the south-east, there were 6,800 Japanese on 16 November, the day the Allied advance commenced. At least 800 were in hospital too ill to be of use – about 20 men a day were dying, mainly from malaria. Another thousand or so convalescents were, in the emergency, given a rifle and a position to hold. Another 2,000 armed men were naval pioneers or civilian construction personnel. Excluding the 800 sick, only half of the 6,000 men available, including the engineers, were combat trained; the rest proved that if what was required was simply to hold a trench unto death, then they would do it.

Blamey advised Herring that speed was imperative, as Japanese reinforcements were on the way, but it was already too late. Within two weeks, 5,000 reinforcements arrived, though not all were fresh. On 17 November, the 700 *144th Regiment* survivors of Oivi–Gorari arrived, and two days later, the 1,450 coming by sea to Buna (mentioned above) landed. On 21 November, 800 men, reinforcements for *41st Regiment* arrived from Rabaul; on 28 November, 700 more from the same regiment came by land. Composing over half of the regiment's survivors of the battle of Oivi–Gorari, the 700 marched down the Kumusi River to the mouth. Then they were ferried to Giruwa. The remainder of the *41st* from Oivi–Gorari, 410 men, remained at the Kumusi and joined with later arrivals to form a new front there, threatening the Australian attack on Gona from the north. On 2 December, a further 900 Japanese came by sea to the Kumusi thence by barge to Giruwa. The final Japanese reinforcements, 591 men, plus a mountain artillery battalion, landed to the north at Mambare River on 14 December. Most were barged into the perimeter at night. In all, 12,000 Japanese were at the battle of Buna–Gona, but probably at no one time did the total number present exceed 11,000, of which around 1,000 were incapacitated by illness or serious wounds – the lightly wounded were patched up and immediately put back into the line. As the Allied strength did not exceed 10,200 at the start of the battle, in the first few weeks the number of defenders roughly equalled the number of attackers.

## AUSTRALIAN FRONT – THE FIRST TWO WEEKS

### *Gona*

On the Gona track, in the north, 25th Brigade encountered the enemy late on 18 November. The next day, 2/31st Battalion attacked south of Gona Mission. The whole brigade, 1,040 strong, about the same number as the defenders, made no impact on the Japanese. The Gona position was 300 yards square, with its right on the river and its rear to the Solomon Sea. While the weakest of all four Japanese fortified areas in terms of bunkers, and containing the fewest number of combat-trained men, it was full of large banyan trees. Their trunks, spreading out like legs, were easily converted into well-protected fighting positions. Originally 900-men strong, on 21 November, 60 men reinforced the garrison and another 80 three days later. Eather prepared a brigade attack on 22 November, but swamps and the Japanese halted it.

With no mortar or artillery support, it was clear there was no chance of a frontal attack working. On 25 November, now with four 25-pdrs to fire 300 rounds before the attack, they tried and failed again. This was the finish of 25th Brigade as an assault formation. It had four battalions, but its total strength was reduced to 750, the size of one battalion. Vasey sent 21st Brigade, the divisional reserve, forward on a new approach. Moving 1,000 yards east of Gona, they reached the sea at Small Creek, eliminating an entrenched Japanese platoon there. On the last day of November, two battalions of the brigade attacked west and east from Small Creek. In the east, 2/14th cleared the coastal track 500 yards towards Basabua, but found it impractical for a later advance on Sanananda as it was underwater at every high tide. The western attack gained only a little ground. That night, 200 men of *41st Regiment* moved along the coast by barge from Giruwa to reinforce Gona but, being unable to find it and fired on by 21st Brigade, they returned.

On 1 December, another assault on Gona was made. This time 2/27th and 2/16th attacked westward from Small Creek through kunai grass, with 3rd Battalion on their left and the sea on their right. The attack, which had artillery support, went awry. As was typical of jungle fighting, 3rd Battalion was not where it thought it was and as such it neither saw the main attack nor itself attacked. A few dozen of 2/16th entered Gona village, where most were killed. The Australians lost 110 men for no gain. The 21st Brigade, already weak, was judged capable of perhaps one more effort before relief.

An Australian company-size force of 2/16th, part of Chaforce, had, since 21 November, held a position west of Gona. Its purpose was to prevent Japanese escaping from Gona, but with the arrival at the mouth of the Kumusi River of *41st Regiment* from Oivi–Gorari, Chaforce's problem became instead to prevent the newcomers breaking into Gona. This they did in a series of skirmishes in the last few days of November and into December against a hungry Japanese force, many of whom had lost their weapons during the retreat.

An Australian 3in mortar crew in action. Judging by the angle of the barrel, they are firing at a target under 200 yards away. (Michael John Claringbould)

## Sanananda

The 16th Brigade, the southern of the two Australian brigades approaching Buna–Gona, was also depleted by two months' fighting in the mountains. On 22 November, 2/3rd Battalion, after briefly clashing with rearguards, found the main Japanese position on the Sanananda road, at the junction of the road and the Cape Killerton track. Held by 700 men of *144th Regiment*, it was a 400-yard-wide circle of bunkers and trenches, with swamp on either side. The brigade went at it, coming under fire from two recently arrived mountain guns. A 90-man company of 2/1st managed to get into the position, throwing back *144th*'s attempts to dislodge it. Overnight, the Japanese contracted their perimeter to accommodate the incursion. One mountain gun was captured.

That was the end of 16th Brigade's offensive capabilities, at least for the moment. It was now the turn of the Americans. As there were more Japanese on Vasey's northern bank of the Giruwa River, the entire 126th Regiment was intended to operate there. However, Colonel Clarence Tomlinson, the regimental commander, retained only the 3/126th, and a 218-man detachment from the 1/126th. The rest of his regiment was taken from him to join 32nd Division south of the river. Tomlinson could count on a little more artillery support as Popondetta strip opened on 21 November and two more 25-pdrs from 2/1st Field Regiment, with 200 rounds, flew in. But the artillery did not change the situation and Tomlinson's advance on 26 November fared as had the Australians. Patrols though found a possible route to the left of the Sanananda road to get into the rear of the Japanese track junction fortification. On 30 November, two companies, 250 men of 126th, found a way along this route, setting up a block on the Sanananda road 1,000 yards north of the Japanese. They dug in and held on against counter-attack at what became known, after its commander, as Huggins roadblock. They also found that there was another Japanese roadblock farther along the road to the coast.

Inside the *144th* position at the road and track junction there was three tons of rice, enough for a slim ration for ten days. After that, it would depend upon whether food could be brought in past Huggins.

## AMERICAN FRONT – THE FIRST TWO WEEKS

### Warren Force

The two American columns south of the Giruwa River were divided by a 2-mile-wide swamp and fought two separate battles until the end of December. Warren Force was on the coast, commanded by Brigadier Hanford MacNider. On 19 November, 1/128th and 3/128th advanced on the coast route, on parallel tracks half a mile apart in pouring rain. Encountering the enemy line on both tracks 3 miles short of Buna Government Station (called Buna Mission at the time), they attacked, with the pitiful support of two old Australian mountain guns, and were stopped cold. Almost no enemy were seen. The men were green, hesitant and unused to the volume of fire directed at them. They could hear trucks behind Japanese lines bringing up reinforcements – the last arrivals of *3/229th*, which had come in by sea the night before. The next day, Lieutenant Colonel Kelsie Miller's 3/128th, on the inland track facing a bridge on Simemi Creek at the western end of New Strip, was so disorganized it could not attack again. It had brought up limited ammunition and this the raw troops had quickly expended. On the coast, Lieutenant Colonel Robert McCoy's 1/128th captured a few enemy outworks on 20 November. Then Lieutenant Colonel Edmund Carrier's 1/126th came forward and attacked on the left of McCoy, whose right was on the sea. Each battalion attacked on a one-company front, 300 yards in all facing north into the Duropa Plantation. The plantation was a 500-yard-wide strip along the coast: solid land with lines of palm trees and less undergrowth, making this the best route to Buna, at least in terms of terrain. Eight hundred yards to the left, Miller would repeat his attempt to capture the Simemi Creek bridge. Between the two, the Australian 2/6th Independent Company provided a link through the swamp.

Papuan carriers preparing to take wounded to Dobodura airstrip, Buna. (Mondadori via Getty Images)

A small bombardment began on 21 November, followed by an air attack, which missed the Japanese, killing or wounding six Americans. Owing to an orders mix-up, the attack did not go in. Later in the day, Allied medium bombers came again, killing or wounding 18 from McCoy's battalion, but no Japanese. The infantry assault got under way a half hour later after a short artillery bombardment, now by four mountain guns and half a dozen mortars. The attack obliged the Japanese to retire from several fighting positions, but their defence system was deep and the Americans had still not reached its main line. On the left, at the bridge, Miller advanced after a 20-round mortar barrage, only to be driven back to his starting point, still 300 yards short of the bridge, with 42 killed and wounded. On 23 November, a massed battery of a dozen 81mm mortars fired against now-known Japanese positions. A 100-yard advance by two companies on the coast brought them, at least there, to the main line of resistance after five days' fighting.

There was a lull of three days to wait for more artillery and shells coming both by sea and by air to newly established strips at Soputa and Dobodura. The attack of 26 November was the first in which any sizeable amount of artillery was available. In addition to the four Australian 3.7in mountain guns, eight 25-pdrs arrived. Four hundred rounds were available. Placed centrally, the guns had the range to support attacks on both sides of the Giruwa River. Three battalions attacked, 3/128th and 1/126th towards Duropa Plantation, with 1/128th in support on the left. A small air attack preceded the assault but, as the men discovered as they advanced against intense fire, neither it nor the artillery had damaged the almost unseen defences. No significant ground was gained. This front along the coast was the most heavily fortified part of the Japanese line and was not cracked until tanks arrived on 18 December.

## Urbana Force

On General Harding's left flank, separated from Warren Force by the 2-mile swamp, was the 2/128th Battalion. It faced the naval component of the Buna defences, 1,050 men under Captain Yasuda Yoshiatsu, mostly *5th Yokosuka* and *5th Sasebo SNLF*. These troops had been shifted westward to prepared defences when *3/229th* and a battalion of *144th* arrived to take over the Duropa Plantation–Old Strip area. Nothing at all was known of Japanese defences here, the most formidable of which was the well-placed Triangle, a 14-bunker complex astride a track junction, the only dry land in the area, where the track divides to lead to Buna village and Buna Government Station. Lieutenant Colonel Herbert Smith, commander of 2/128th, encountering firm resistance at the Triangle, flanked into the swamp westward. He requested and was granted the aid of 2/126th, then situated across the Giruwa River on the Australian front. The battalion reached Smith on 23 November, the two battalions taking the name Urbana Force, under command of Colonel John Mott. Feeling leftward along Entrance Creek, the Americans found it unfordable. While Urbana's far left, towards the creek mouth and Buna village, looked promising, the only way to supply troops there was by carrying parties leaving the track before the Triangle and passing through deep swamp. The farther left (north-west) they progressed, the harder it was to get food and ammunition to them.

An attack on the Triangle on 24 November failed and it seemed to Mott that a move towards Buna village on the left, accepting the problem of supply there, might yield better results. There was a three-day lull and on 30 November the attack was renewed. On the far left, a company reached the coastal track west of Buna Government Station, cutting Japanese communications between the Sanananda–Giruwa central position and the Buna–Cape Endiadere eastern position, preventing reinforcements coming by land, if not by sea.

Heralding the return of the IJN to Papuan skies, Aichi D3A Vals and A6M Zeros from Lae began a series of bombing and strafing attacks on Dobodura, attempting to cut Allied air supply. On 27 November, Zeros hit ammunition dumps and hospitals at Soputa, killing 28 and wounding 50 Australians and Americans.

# THE *COUP DE MAIN* FAILS

By the first few days of December not a lot had been accomplished from the perspective of Allied high command – a perspective which hoped the whole Japanese position would have been taken by now. Gona was cut off and, on the Sanananda track, Huggins roadblock was in place. South of the Giruwa River, the Japanese line had been uncovered, but nowhere penetrated, though the Japanese coastal route at Buna village was cut. However, all four Japanese positions remained intact. The Allied attempt to take the beachhead on the run, by *coup de main*, had failed.

From the Japanese perspective, the first two weeks were a success. They noted that no vital part of the perimeter had been captured – it was not until 5 December when the Americans cut off Buna village from the Government Station that the Japanese thought their enemy had made any serious progress. The 2,000 survivors of the battle at Oivi–Gorari had either escaped to Buna, or were north of Gona posing a threat to the Australian left. Arrivals by sea, with food and ammunition, had thus far come without much interference. It appeared that the entire Buna–Gona fortress could comfortably hold, provided a minimum of supplies continued to come by sea.

## COMMAND

An attacker with no significant numerical superiority, sometimes none at all; little help from field artillery or mortars; airpower yet to learn close support in the jungle; worn out troops on the Australian front; green ones on the American front, faced a well dug-in determined enemy. The attackers failed to make an impact – not a surprising result. As a consequence, Allied morale plummeted on the battlefield and at headquarters.

In Port Moresby, MacArthur was alarmed. In two weeks, 32nd Division had lost 492 men in battle, as many as that to disease, and had little to show for it. On top of this, reports came back of Americans throwing away their weapons and running, and of attacks ordered not being made. MacArthur had been critical of the Australian performance on the Kokoda Trail, now it was Blamey's turn. Reinforcements were called for because of unexpectedly strong Japanese opposition. MacArthur wanted to send the US 41st Division, but Blamey said he would prefer more Australians as he 'knew they would fight'. As there were twice as many Americans present in November, and there were more Japanese north of the Giruwa River on the Australian front, Blamey expected the Americans to shoulder the main burden, including contributing more troops to the Australian sector. While his criticism of the poor quality of 32nd Division had merit, it can in part be offset by the fact that the Americans faced the densest Japanese defences and the freshest Japanese troops. Even so, as Blamey pointed out, the Americans outnumbered their opponents south of the Giruwa River by at very least 2:1, while the Australians faced tougher odds north of the river.

MacArthur decided to replace Harding. He sent Lieutenant General Robert Eichelberger, 1st Corps commander, to Buna. MacArthur, at his dramatic best, said, 'I want you to take Buna Bob, or don't come back alive.' On 2 December, after a day inspecting the front during an attack, Eichelberger relieved Harding. Later he fired six regimental and battalion commanders. Eichelberger was now in effect a divisional commander under Herring.

The Japanese had a reshuffle too. Hyakutake had been in Guadalcanal for six weeks, attempting to run both that battle and Papua. Chief of the Army General Staff at IHQ, General Sugiyama Hajime, realized it was not working. He arranged a change. From 26 November, Hyakutake's *17th Army* would be solely responsible for Guadalcanal. A new *18th Army*, under Lieutenant General Adachi Hatazo, took over Papua and New Guinea, while a new *8th Area Army* under General Imamura Hitoshi, who had commanded the very successful invasion of the Dutch East Indies, oversaw both from Rabaul. Unlike command changes on the Allied side, no one was sacked. Imamura, seeing the weakness of the initial Allied assault on Buna–Gona, pushed for reinforcements for Papua, the *21st Mixed Brigade*. He entertained hopes of a large-scale counter-attack to drive off the Allies. This reinforcement undercut the Japanese strategy to put Papua on hold while Guadalcanal was won, but IHQ was still in its last weeks of optimism, believing both could be held. It granted Imamura's request.

# The battle of Buna–Gona, 10 December 1942–22 January 1943

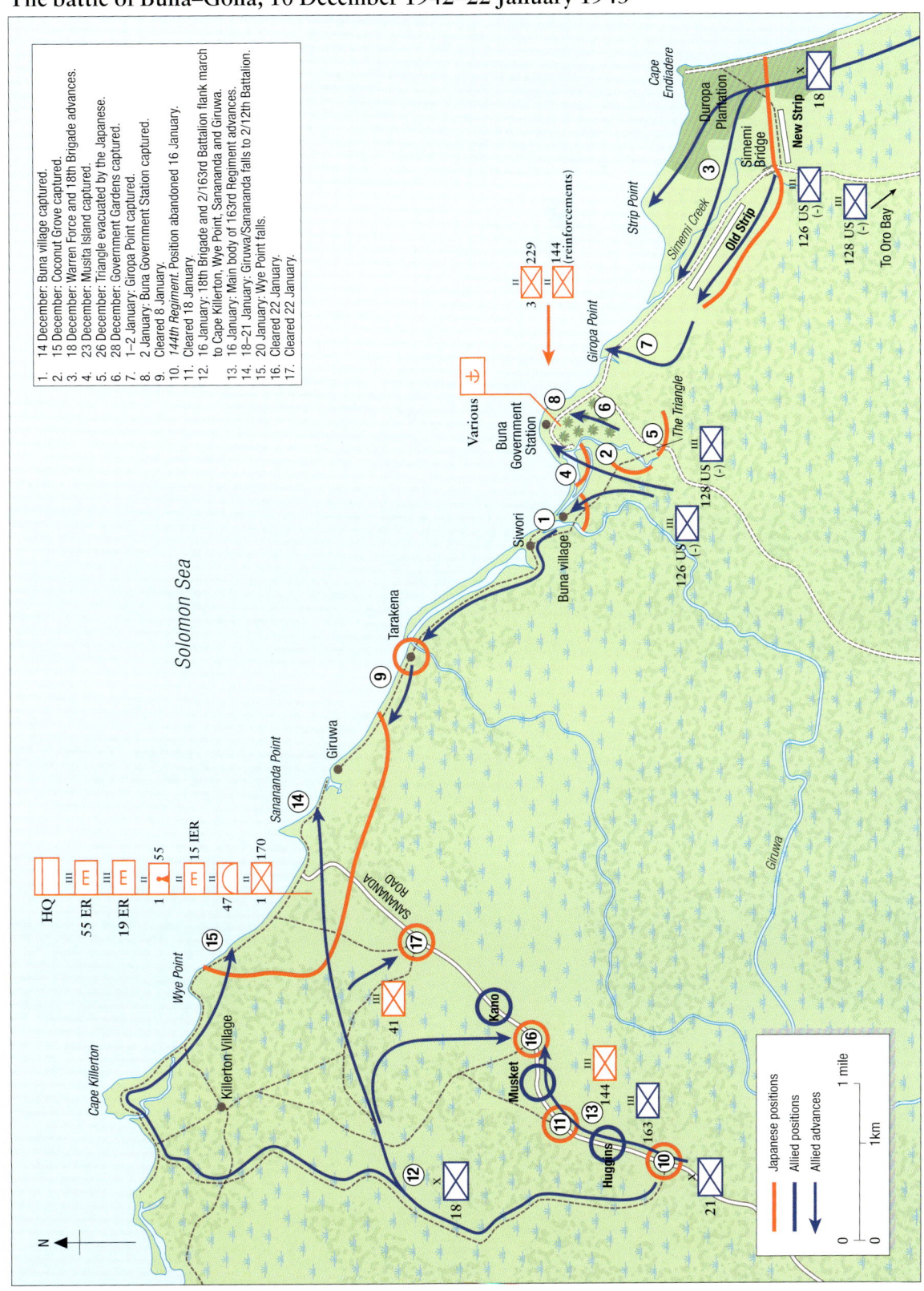

The *21st Mixed Brigade*, under Major General Yamagata Tsuyou's orders, was to launch an offensive against the Australians first, then sweep southward and capture the airstrips at Dobodura. Unable to land at Basabua, he came ashore at the Kumusi River mouth with one battalion, 10 miles north-west of Buna, on 1 December, taking command of the entire Japanese force on the coast. A further battalion and artillery, the last reinforcement to get through, arrived on 14 December, having to land even farther north, at the Mambare River, 35 miles north-west of Buna. Owing to the failure of all intended reinforcements to arrive, and the dispersion of those that did, Yamagata's offensive never took place. In a matter of days, the optimism which had prompted the sending of *21st Mixed Brigade* to Buna was gone. IHQ began to discuss withdrawing from Papua. On 12 December, before the 14 December convoy had even left Rabaul, Adachi was informally told the withdrawal from Papua would probably occur in the not too distant future.

## WARREN FRONT IN DECEMBER

The two main Japanese positions, at the bridge on Simemi Creek and in the Duropa Plantation, were as firmly held as before. All US battalions were reduced by a third by casualties and sickness, and rations were down to 1,200 calories per day; fighting troops needed 4,000. The 127th RCT, the third regiment of 32nd Division, now at Port Moresby, could not be brought forward until it could be fed. There were no tents to shelter from the constant rain or broiling sun. There was no quinine for malaria suppression until the last day of November. There was no sign of tanks or rifle grenades to aid in bunker busting. A flamethrower was tried on 8 December, but it did not work.

On 3 December, five Australian Bren carriers arrived. With a half inch of armour and open tops, these were no substitute for tanks, but were all that could be brought forward by sea. Colonel Clarence Martin, one of Eichelberger's staff officers, was now in command on the Warren front. He decided to use

The Australian 2/9th Battalion during the 18 December attack on the Duropa Plantation. A Japanese bunker is on the left. (Michael John Claringbould)

the Bren carriers on the good ground in Duropa Plantation. Arriving in luggers with the Bren carriers was 40 tons of food and ammunition: Warren Force had run out of rations that day. Eichelberger ordered a three-battalion attack for 5 December: Colonel Edmund Carrier's 1/126th on the left at Simemi Creek bridge, the 2/6th Independent Company to their right, then McCoy in the centre and Miller on the right on the coast. Half a dozen A-20s bombed the Japanese, then artillery and mortars opened fire. The Bren carriers and infantry advanced through the comparatively open ground of the plantation. Within 15 minutes, all five carriers were knocked out, two-thirds of their crews were casualties, while the infantry gained just 40 yards. As Colonel Martin put it, 'we have hit them and bounced off'. That day Herring told Eichelberger means had been found to bring tanks forward and a fresh, veteran brigade of Australians would be with them. Considering this day's failure on the Warren front, Eichelberger decided to wait for them. The fighting here settled down to a siege until the tanks arrived.

Inside a typical Japanese bunker at Buna. (Bradley Collection)

Seven M3 Stuart tanks from 2/6th Australian Armoured Regiment came with 18th Australian Infantry Brigade, veterans of Tobruk and Milne Bay. Their commander, Brigadier George Wootten, took charge of the Warren front. Wootten, a Gallipoli, Western Front and Middle East veteran was, according to MacArthur, 'the best the Australians had'. After a bombardment on 18 December, now with 14 guns, 2/9th of Wootten's brigade, with M3 tanks in support, attacked north through the plantation. Tanks and fresh war-hardened troops made all the difference. Supported by 3/128th and an element of 1/128th, 2/9th smashed through the Japanese line, the tanks dealing with pillboxes and bunkers, some with 4ft-thick coconut log roofs and 6ft-thick front walls. They advanced 900 yards to Cape Endiadere in an hour, then the attack turned to the west. Two tanks were knocked out and one-third of the Australians were casualties, but the Japanese line was broken on a 500-yard front. In the following two days, 2/9th and 2/10th Battalions, with US infantry support, cleared the Japanese from other positions east of Simemi Creek.

US infantry at Cape Endiadere, 21 December 1942. (SC 166707, public domain, via Signal Corps Archive on Flickr)

By 20 December, the entire east bank of Simemi Creek was cleared. Old Strip was the next objective. On 21 December, 2/10th and 1/126th captured the Simemi bridge area and drove north-west 800 yards up Old Strip. The Simemi Creek bridge, 125ft long over swamp and creek, was repaired by engineers for tanks to cross to attack Old Strip.

**ATTACK AT DUROPA PLANTATION, 18 DECEMBER 1942 (PP. 76–77)**

On 18 December 1942, the fresh 18th Australian Brigade, with tanks in support, was committed to the Warren front. Its 2/9th Battalion, last in action at Milne Bay in August, attacked north through the Duropa Plantation **(1)**. The battalion overran the Japanese line which had held for a month, reaching Cape Endiadere.

The 3/128th Battalion **(2)** was given the task of following the 2/9th and mopping up bypassed concealed Japanese positions. Far more Japanese were encountered than expected, the battalion taking until dark to finish the task.

Japanese bunkers **(3)**, which contained from 10 to 30 men, were intended to provide protection from artillery and aerial bombardment, after which the infantry would leave the bunkers through a network of trenches to their fighting positions. On 18 December, many Japanese were driven back into their bunkers where they were eliminated by close range 37mm high explosive rounds fired by the tanks.

This attack saw the first use of tanks **(4)** at the battle of Buna–Gona. Seven M3 Stuart light tanks were committed from C Squadron, 2/6th Australian Armoured Regiment. The Japanese had no anti-tank guns in the Duropa Plantation. Two tanks were lost, one when a Japanese soldier attached a magnetic mine to it.

The 2/9th Battalion suffered 55 dead and 117 wounded **(5)**, one-third of those engaged. Casualties for 3/128th were six killed and 23 wounded.

On 24 December, the attack went forward 500 yards, but two of the three tanks were knocked out by a 75mm gun on Old Strip operating in an anti-tank role. On Christmas Day and the next, 1/126th advanced up the west side of Old Strip, the Australians on the east side. A 25-pdr with armour piercing shells was brought forward to destroy each bunker as located with direct fire, helping the advance on 27 December. Within ten days of the first attack with tanks, the Australian–American line was 2,500 yards farther north-west. Along with late December successes on Urbana front, the remaining Japanese south of the Giruwa were now restricted to a coastal strip 400 yards wide and 2,200 yards long, from the mouth of Simemi Creek to Buna Government Station.

More tanks arriving aided a small advance on 29 December, when there was a pause as the last of Wootten's 18th Brigade battalions, 2/12th, came forward to spearhead an attack towards Giropa Point on New Year's Day.

Bridge over Simemi Creek built by 32nd Division engineers to enable tanks to attack at Old Strip a few days later. (History and Art Collection/Alamy Stock Photo)

## URBANA FRONT IN DECEMBER

On 4 December, Colonel Tomlinson transferred his headquarters to Urbana, where the majority of his regiment was now situated. The next day, with 2/126th Battalion on his left, they attacked Buna village. On the right 2/128th closed up along Entrance Creek, working its way behind the Triangle. A nine-aircraft B-25 strike, ten 81mm mortars and a 37mm gun with cannister rounds were in support. Open ground around the entrenched village stopped the advance 50 yards short of the huts. However, to the right (east) of the village, one platoon, under Sergeant Herman Bottcher, broke through to the sea. This was the first Allied advance to concern Yamagata. Two days of Japanese counter-attacks by *5th Sasebo*, ordered by Yasuda, failed to eject the platoon. Yasuda now had 585 IJN men remaining on Urbana front of the 1,050 he had had at the start of the battle. His western flank, Buna village, was already cut off from Giruwa, now his eastern flank was cut off from Buna Government Station. While the Warren front was relatively quiet after the failure of 5 December, Urbana remained active. The 2/128th now held all the west side of Entrance Creek, except for Coconut Grove, another Japanese strongpoint. Attacks on Buna village on 6 and 7 December failed.

Reinforcements were at hand. With 126th and 128th Regiments now depleted (2/126th, the weakest battalion, was down to 250 men), the fresh third regiment of 32nd Division began to arrive. The 3/127th Battalion, under Lieutenant Colonel Edwin Swedberg, came by air to Dobodura and Popondetta with 900 men. Three days later, on 14 December, 3/127th attacked the now isolated Buna village after

Men of 127th Infantry Regiment under fire near Buna Government Station, 28 December. (SC 171587, public domain, via Signal Corps Archive on Flickr)

SS *Karsik*, which brought tanks to Buna. Before a course through coral reefs was charted, only small coastal vessels could bring cargo to Oro Bay, the main Allied supply point on the coast 11 miles south of the nearest Japanese positions. (Australian War Memorial 303479)

a 400-mortar-round bombardment. The 100 remaining Japanese were gone, evacuated by sea at night to Giruwa.

The next Urbana objective was Coconut Grove, the only Japanese position left west of Entrance Creek. A two-company attack, on 15 December, comprising 105 men of 2/128th with mortar support, was surprisingly successful. The grove was taken and 37 bodies found at a cost of four killed and 14 wounded. The 2/128th immediately established a small bridgehead across Entrance Creek. Possession of Coconut Grove and the bridgehead offered a new approach to the rear of the Triangle, but attacks on 17 and 18 December failed.

On the Urbana left, a company of 126th crossed the Giruwa River on 16 December, advancing a mile and a half to Tarakena, keeping the Japanese at Giruwa at arm's length. On 20 December, the Americans were pushed back, the line settling down 300 yards south-east of Tarakena village.

As supply improved in December, the rest of the 127th arrived and elements of the 126th and 128th RCTs not at first present, such as engineers, had dribbled in. With losses thus far of 667 killed or wounded and 1,260 evacuated sick, the fresh regiment of 2,734 men brought US numbers up to about 8,500, possibly the highest number present at any one time.

On 19 December, two weak companies of 2/126th attacked the Triangle from the north-west, out of the bridgehead on the east side of Entrance Creek. Air again was in support, and again wounded Americans – after 22 December, 32nd Division, having lost 35 killed and wounded to their own aircraft, declined to ask for more direct support missions. One of the difficulties was lack of air-to-ground communication. On no occasion had a pilot been in direct contact with the troops he was supporting. Close air support was in any case small. A mere 121 sorties had been flown thus far with only 40 tons of bombs dropped. The bombing of Japanese rear areas continued, but close air support preparatory to attacks was abandoned.

A Wirraway from No 4 Squadron RAAF, spotting for artillery. (Historic Collection/Alamy Stock Photo)

The two-company attack achieved nothing. Two more attempts at the Triangle were made that day, the last preceded by an unusually strong mortar bombardment, 700 rounds from 20 mortars. The attack failed with the loss of 40 killed and wounded from 107 men. Two more attacks made on the Triangle on 20 December cost 39 casualties for no gain. The 2/126th was placed in reserve while the 127th Regiment took over its lines as well as most of the Urbana front. That day, Colonel John Grose, commander of 127th, took over Urbana from Tomlinson. After a dozen unsuccessful attacks and 240 casualties in attempts to capture the Triangle, Eichelberger ruled that it be bypassed; Herring agreed. The major effort of Urbana would now be directed at Buna Government Station. One avenue of approach was across Entrance Creek, north

A US 37mm gun positioned at Musita Island (called simply 'the Island' during the battle) to fire on Buna Government Station. (PJF Military Collection/Alamy Stock Photo)

of the Triangle through Government Gardens. An attack in the dark on the morning of 22 December saw 75 men across, at a cost of 54 casualties, creating another bridgehead 300 yards north of the one that had enabled the recent attacks on the Triangle.

On 23 December, Musita Island was captured, after a failure a few days previously. A 37mm gun was placed on its north side to fire on Buna Government Station.

At dawn on 27 December, 3/127th attacked out of the new bridgehead on Entrance Creek on a 400-yard front. Eight hundred yards would take them to the sea through the well-bunkered, now overgrown Government Gardens,

US infantry clearing a Japanese bunker. Note the crawl trench leading from the bunker to a network of fighting positions around the bunker. (PJF Military Collection/Alamy Stock Photo)

A Japanese soldier, trying to escape by sea near Cape Endiadere, is called upon to surrender. He held a grenade to his head and, moments after the photograph was taken, it exploded, 28 December 1942. (History and Art Collection/Alamy Stock Photo)

with a 100-yard swamp in the middle. The *5th SNLF* with armed naval pioneers were in defence. Only small gains were made. On Christmas Day, 127th attacked into Government Gardens again, taking a slim salient 250 yards from the sea and 600 yards east of Government Station. Repeated efforts brought the 127th to within 100 yards of the sea there. Yasuda shifted troops to meet each new attack. His line stretched thin, but did not break anywhere. However, the Triangle would be totally cut off once the Americans crossed the last hundred yards to the sea. Yasuda ordered its evacuation.

By 28 December, 3/127th had gained that last 100 yards, cutting the coast track east of Buna Government Station. The remaining Japanese in the Buna area were now in two pockets: a 400 by 400 yard position at Buna Government Station, and a 1,400-yard by 400-yard strip between where 127th had driven its wedge through Government Gardens to the sea, and the mouth of Simemi Creek in the Warren front area of operations. After six weeks fighting two distinct battles, Urbana and Warren fronts were about to link up.

## DECEMBER ON THE AUSTRALIAN FRONT

### Gona

On 2 December, 30th Brigade began to arrive. Its 39th Battalion was committed to the Gona front where 21st Brigade had lost 430 casualties in five days and was to be withdrawn. Four days later, Gona was again attacked with 2/16th and 2/27th, now organized as a composite battalion, attacking westward with the 39th coming from the south. The attack appeared to have achieved nothing, but the Japanese were near the end. Perhaps 200, one-fifth of the garrison, were still alive. When Brigadier Ivan Dougherty, commander 21st Brigade, attacked again on 8 December, after 15 minutes of artillery preparation and air support, 39th Battalion broke into Gona village from the south-east as the composite battalion also broke the line on the east side of the village. That night, most of the remaining Japanese attempted a breakout; a third got away to Sanananda. The following day, vicious mopping up captured the last Japanese position. Gona, one of the four fortified areas, had fallen. Around 950 Japanese died there, including the garrison commander, Major Yamamoto Tsunichi. The Australians, who at no time numbered more than 1,400, took 757 casualties. On the last day at Gona, a 2/16th patrol reported dealing with 12 Japanese of whom nine were 'stretcher cases', who nevertheless fired on them until they were killed.

On 6 December, the Chaforce blocking position of 20 men north-west of Gona was almost wiped out by *41st Regiment*. The Japanese here consisted of *1/41st Battalion*, 300 survivors of Oivi–Gorari who had been left behind when the bulk of the regiment was transferred by barge into the perimeter.

After Gona fell, 39th and 2/14th Battalions were sent into this area between Gona and the Amboga River. In a week's fighting, they recaptured Haddy's village, as the outermost Chaforce position was known, and advanced to the river, securing the Allied left flank.

## *Sanananda*

On the Sanananda road, with Huggins roadblock behind the main Japanese position, the supply predicament for both sides was doubled. Both had to send supplies through the swamp on either side of the enemy. As each discovered the other's supply route, they attempted to cut it. As the Japanese could not take Huggins and the Americans and Australians could not take the *144th* roadblock on the junction between Sanananda road and Cape Killerton track, it was a matter of who could last the longest.

Porter's two battalions of 30th Brigade, untried militia, relieved 16th Brigade on the Sanananda road. Porter's attack on 7 December failed badly after the best artillery and mortar preparation seen on this front. It was a disaster, losing 229 men in three hours, an attack reminiscent of earlier US efforts where, as Porter complained, inexperience caused high casualties without success.

On 8 and 10 December, supply parties got through to Huggins. The day in between, a Japanese party snuck through supplies to *144th Regiment* in the southernmost of the Japanese roadblocks. In the following 12 days, no attacks were made as a recent arrival, 2/7th Cavalry Regiment, made its way through swamp to Huggins to relieve the garrison. On 19 December, a new round of attacks began up the road with the 49th on the right and 55/53rd on the left. The 36th Battalion was in reserve to exploit any success. There were four guns in support. The attack failed with the exception that 49th Battalion turned the Japanese flank on the east side, creating a fairly secure supply line to Huggins. Meanwhile, 2/7th struck north along the Sanananda road out of Huggins. There it bumped into the previously established Japanese position a few hundred yards north. It was held by 700 fresh replacements for *41st Regiment*, which had been formed into a separate battalion. The 2/7th skirted this and established Kano, yet another roadblock behind the Japanese. The Japanese in turn blocked the track a little farther towards the coast.

The situation now was an extremely unusual one. In the south across the road were the Australians and Americans, facing the original Japanese position on the junction of Sanananda road and the Cape Killerton track. North of that was Huggins, then the Japanese *41st Regiment* block, then Kano, then more Japanese to the north of that, all along 2,500 yards of the narrow causeway of ground just above swamp level along the Sanananda road. All these defences, except the Japanese one in the north and the Allied one in the south, depended for supply on carrying parties finding their way through swamp on the flanks. With two roadblocks behind it, the southernmost Japanese position was now isolated. No more supplies came through. On 22 December, 39th Battalion arrived after the fighting on the Amboga River. Despite being given more men, Vasey opted for a temporary stalemate.

The 2/7th Australian Cavalry Regiment in a Sanananda swamp, December 1942. (Australian War Memorial 013971)

Wounded soldier of 32nd Division at Buna, December 1942. (Michael John Claringbould)

With about 1,600 men against 1,200 Japanese along the Sanananda road there was, he believed, no prospect of success at that moment.

## SUPPLY

At the end of December, *144th Regiment* on the Sanananda road was entirely cut off. These men were starving and some resorted to cannibalism. The majority of Japanese within their fortress, however, still had food and ammunition, though a ration could be as low as a few hundred calories a day. The problem was distribution of food as a result of Allied penetrations. Those men at the outer edge of the Japanese fortifications starved, those close to supply dumps did not. Some remained well fed, many were malnourished, but only a minority were starving.

North of Gona, the force on the coast between Amboga and Mambare rivers received at least 80 tons of supplies from the sea by destroyers and submarines from mid-December to 14 January, though coastwatchers reported arrivals, which aircraft and PT boats sometimes intercepted. Little coral in the northern approach to Buna and better naval charts made night-time runs easier for the Japanese than the coral-strewn Allied sea route from Milne Bay. A portion of the Mambare supplies trickled down the coast at night to Sanananda and Buna on eight Daihatsu barges. In the central position of Sanananda–Giruwa, but not out on the Sanananda road, the situation was best. With the return of IJN air after several months focused on Guadalcanal, supplies were airdropped, 40 tons each on 4 and 10 December and submarines dropped off various cargo three times in mid-December. At Buna, there was still some food, ammunition and medical supplies left when the Allies captured Japanese positions. A ton of rice was found within the Triangle. Similar dumps, including medical supplies, were found by the Americans when they captured Buna Government Station and Buna village.

The Allied supply line to Buna, by air and sea, hovered on the brink of collapse, but never actually did. A bare minimum of 60 tons was supposed to be delivered each day; 25 flights or two coastal barges' worth. Ninety tons was desired if a 21-day reserve was to be built up. This was never achieved. Several times heavy rain halted all air transport, as occurred from 19 to 21 November. On the other hand, transport aircraft were still increasing in number – personnel movement by air, for example, casualties out and reinforcements in, jumped from 2,280 in November to 8,881 in December.

General Harding's problems in November stemmed from an inadequate supply line. It prevented him getting the additional infantry regiment, food, ammunition, artillery and tanks he asked for. Within two weeks of Harding's relief, the supply line's capacity was doubled both by air and sea. On 14 December, a record 178 tons of cargo came in by air. The jeep roads from four airfields to the fronts were also much improved. By now, Royal Australian Navy hydrographers had marked a channel through the reefs off Cape Nelson, permitting large transports to bring tanks and guns to Oro Bay. Much of what Harding had asked for in November arrived to benefit Eichelberger in December.

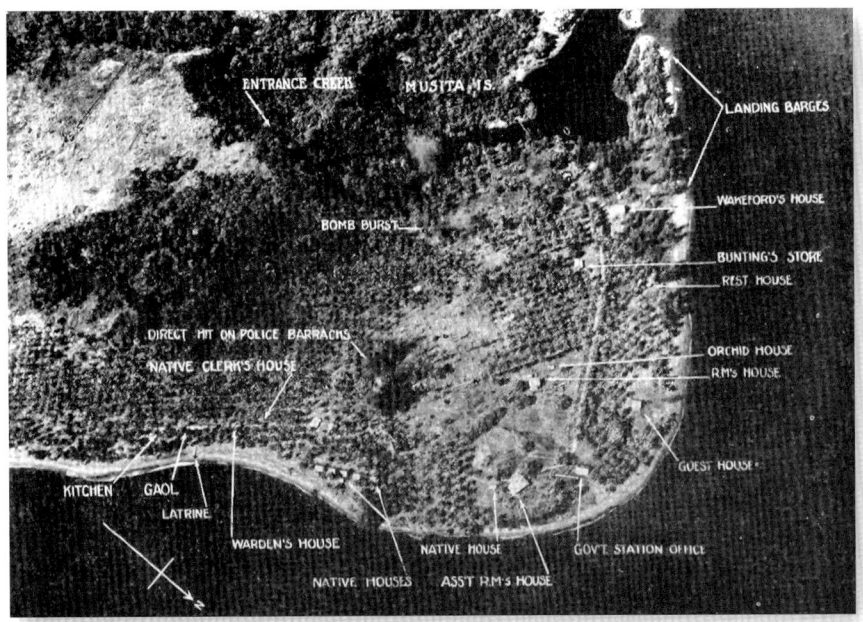

Aerial photograph of Buna Government Station before its capture. (Public domain via Wikimedia Commons)

## JANUARY ON THE AMERICAN FRONT

Owing to the Warren front's almost 2-mile advance over the previous 13 days, since 18 December, the Urbana units in Government Gardens were now only a few hundred yards from and in patrol contact with the Warren front troops. On 31 December, Urbana Force attacked Buna Government Station from Musita Island, achieving a bridgehead close to it. On New Year's Day, 2/12th, with six tanks, and 1/128th and 3/128th following to mop up, attacked northward across Old Strip to Giropa Point on a 400-yard front, two companies up and two back, taking on the last Japanese position east of Buna Station.

Vickers machine guns in support of the 2/12th Battalion's attack on Giropa Point, 1 January 1943. (Bradley Collection)

A thin strip of coconut palms by the sea, 500 yards away, was reached in 30 minutes, splitting the defenders in two. Tanks made short work of Japanese bunkers and trenches. That night, in a lightning storm, escaping Japanese were shot down. The next day, the two pockets were eliminated. At the same time, 127th moved west along the coast for Buna Government Station, the last Japanese bastion, which was reduced by the evening of 2 January. In the Station, Captain Yasuda and Colonel Yamamoto committed seppuku.

Adachi, in Rabaul – Imamura refused him permission to go to Buna – had ordered Yamagata to evacuate what was left of the Buna position on 26 December. A rescue force of 230 men from *1/170th Battalion*, which had been held in reserve at Giruwa, was assembled, but did not attack towards Buna until it was all over. They did manage to gather in 370

2/12th Battalion Bren gunners and 2/6th Armoured Regiment tank fire on a Japanese bunker, Giropa Point, 1 January 1943. (Australian War Memorial 014001)

men, all who survived from the Buna–Cape Endiadere garrison, apart from the 100 who had escaped from Buna village earlier and 70 who were captured.

The only remaining task, now that Urbana and the Warren front had joined, was to contribute to the fall of Giruwa–Sanananda, 2 miles to the north-west. Tarakena was cleared on 8 January, then the advance was held up by *1/170th Battalion*. The advance resumed on 19 January. The next day 127th was in sight of Giruwa, where they could see Australian patrols in the village.

On the American front south of the Giruwa River, the Allied cost was 2,870 battle casualties, 913 of them Australian. Some 1,390 Japanese dead were counted. In fact, at least 2,100 Japanese were killed in the fighting there.

## JANUARY ON THE AUSTRALIAN FRONT

North of Giruwa River, the Australian front received the last of four American infantry regiments to fight in Papua, the 163rd of 41st Division. Which side of the Giruwa River would take command of the incoming regiment was a cause of friction between the Allies. However, with the end at Buna in sight, Herring gave the 163rd to the Australians. Deplaning at Popondetta on 30 December, the 1/163rd took over the Sanananda roadblocks on 2 January. The next battalion, 2/163rd, arrived a week later and secured the supply line to the roadblocks north of the *144th*, which was still holding the Killerton track junction. On 10 January, 3/163rd reached the front, took over Kano and established yet another Sanananda roadblock called Musket.

32nd Division dead at Buna. (Bettmann via Getty Images)

General Vasey's plan now was, when 18th Brigade arrived from the US sector, for 2/163rd to place a roadblock on Killerton track, to further isolate *144th Regiment*. The 18th Brigade and 2/7th Cavalry, with 2/6th Armoured Regiment, would attack down the Sanananda road as far as Huggins. Then 163rd would continue the drive to Sanananda, while 18th Brigade would swing left, coming at Sanananda from the west. On 9 January, 2/163rd set up a block on the Killerton track. Meanwhile, 1/163rd attacked the Japanese between Huggins and Kano. These operations, and the capture of Buna Government Station, convinced the commanders that only mopping up remained. MacArthur returned to Australia and Herring to Port Moresby, while Eichelberger took over Herring's job in command of all troops on the north coast of Papua.

Japanese dead on the beach at Buna Government Station, January 1942. (Photo 12/ Universal Images Group via Getty Images)

On 12 January, 18th Brigade, having marched from Old Strip to the Sanananda road, taking in 800 replacements along the way, attacked directly down the road, the only suitable ground for their three tanks. A Japanese field gun operating in the anti-tank role quickly knocked out all the tanks and the attack ground to a halt. Japanese artillery had insufficient ammunition for anything but the direct fire role, against tanks or infantry. At no time during the battle did it worry the Allies with an indirect bombardment. Vasey decided on no more attacks here. Instead, he would pound the Japanese with the increasing amounts of artillery rounds available now there was no need for artillery south of the Giruwa River.

Within the track junction, Tsukamoto, commander of *144th*, saw things differently. Out of contact with his superiors, he decided that his starving men could not withstand another assault and withdrew westward on the night of 16 January. Leaving behind the sick and wounded, 300 men slipped through the swamps, attempting to avoid contact. Only 140 arrived at the Kumusi River mouth several days later. Learning of the evacuation, the Australians took the track junction, held only by men too weak to move, none of whom surrendered. The next day, the constant rain of the previous six weeks ended. Tracks began to dry and swamps become shallower, aiding the Allied advance. By 18 January, the Sanananda road was cleared all the way to Huggins.

The 18th Brigade resumed the plan to swing west and go for Sanananda via Cape Killerton, while 2/163rd advanced up the road. On 16 January 2/10th got to Cape Killerton unopposed, drove east towards Sanananda, but was held up by Japanese defences at Wye Point. The 163rd was also halted farther along the Sanananda road . The next day 2/12th went straight through a deep swamp, directly to Sanananda, capturing it by assault on 18 January. The Australians were surprised to find the positions along the coast at Sanananda and Giruwa were not as strongly held as they expected. It was plain the Japanese defences were falling apart. The last four large pockets of resistance, Giruwa, Wye Point and two pockets on the Sanananda road, were reduced in the period 17–22 January. Small and large dumps of ammunition and food were found in all these places.

## BREAKOUT

The sudden collapse of resistance was a result of the Japanese breakout, which the Allies did not realize was occurring. A month earlier, IHQ had decided Papua could not be held, but did not order a withdrawal immediately. Now, early in January, Imamura was told to make a phased withdrawal, the timing to be determined in Rabaul. Imamura had Adachi order Yamagata to start the evacuation on 25 January. As this was much too late, Yamagata acted immediately. The evacuation of 1,190 sick and wounded to the Mambare River began and plans were drawn up for a breakout on 20 January.

Additional barges were sent from Rabaul, giving 18 in all with a carrying capacity of 1,260 men, or a quarter of that number of wounded. The sick and wounded who could not be evacuated were instructed to take their own lives.

Adachi's plan was that the force, having cut their way out by land or moved by sea in barges, would first assemble in the Kumusi–Mambare area, then proceed by sea 120 miles to Lae.

The breakout commenced in the early evening of 20 January. Yamagata left the day before, but others, like Major General Oda Kensaku, commander of the *Nankai Shitai* under Yamagata, stayed to commit suicide. The rest divided into platoon-sized units and moved west on a wide front from Cape Killerton to Soputa. There were numerous small clashes with Australians and the PIB that patrolled north of Gona. Japanese estimates are that 550 were killed in the breakout. As planned the remainder gathered at Mambare before moving by night up the coast to Lae, where the last of them arrived late in February.

## SUMMING UP

US medics treat a wounded Australian, January 1943. (SuperStock/Alamy Stock Photo)

The battle of Buna–Gona was the first time in the war in the Pacific that such elaborate defences, constructed over four months, had been encountered by the Allies. It represented a significant learning experience for them. The reason for the failure of almost all Allied assaults up to 18 December was a lack of artillery, for which the tanks available from that day forward somewhat compensated. From late November, four or six guns were in support of a battalion- or regiment-sized attack, in December a dozen. For a corps-level operation, admittedly a small corps, this was far from enough, and there was never sufficient ammunition. Preparatory bombardments at Buna were typically allocated 200–400 rounds, while at Guadalcanal, where naval gunfire support was also sometimes available, 8,883 rounds were fired by field artillery

Japanese prisoners of war after the battle of Buna–Gona. (Michael John Claringbould)

on 23 October 1942 alone. At Buna, the Allies never had more than 20 guns in action; by 2 January, at Guadalcanal, with a fighting force twice as large, there were 167 guns.

Some 15,000 Americans were at Buna–Gona at one time or another from November to January. Nine hundred and thirty of these died in the battle and 1,918 were wounded. A further 7,920 were 'sick in action', most of whom were evacuated. The Americans had very few replacements in Australia to send, resulting in units dwindling rapidly in size from battle casualties and disease. The 126th RCT, the hardest hit, entered battle with 3,171 men and came out with 611. Several of its companies were down to 14 or 15 men.

The Australian units, in contrast, entered the battle weak in strength, but had a replacement system in place and were able to send 2,200 replacements to their various brigades. Eleven thousand Australians were at the battle, but not more than 6,000 at one time. Their casualties were 1,261 dead from all battle causes, with 2,219 wounded. There were 4,100 sick, most of whom were evacuated.

There were 12,000 Japanese at Buna–Gona, about 4,800 of them still alive at the time of the breakout. Of these, 1,200 wounded and sick were evacuated by barge, 800 had always been north of Gona so easily retreated to Mambare, and about 1,100 successfully broke through the Australian lines and made their way north. In all, 3,105 assembled at the Mambare River in early February. The remainder died, excepting 260 prisoners of war.

Japanese Type 88 75mm gun captured at Buna. (Australian War Memorial P03664.001)

# AFTERMATH

The Papuan Campaign was the last Japanese invasion in the Pacific. Their retreat from Ioribaiwa Ridge on the Kokoda Trail in September 1942 marks, together with Milne Bay, the end of ten months on the offensive and the beginning of almost three years defending their Pacific gains. The loss of Buna made it plain to the IJN that Rabaul could not be, as intended, the southern seas version of Truk, their premier navy base outside Japan.

When defeat in Papua was clearly imminent, in the midst of the battle of Buna–Gona, the Japanese tried to establish a new defence line between Wau and Salamaua, 120 miles north-west of Buna in the Territory of New Guinea. On 16 January, a week before the end at Buna–Gona, Imamura sent *102nd Infantry Regiment* from Salamaua to secure Wau. It was forestalled by the Australians, who flew a brigade into Wau in time to hold the airstrip, then force back the Japanese. The new defensive line adopted was Lae, and it was an attempted reinforcement of Lae that resulted in the battle of the Bismarck Sea in March 1943, when the Japanese convoy was sunk by air attack, many of the aircraft flying out of Dobodura.

The expulsion of the Japanese from Papua six months after they first landed there enabled MacArthur to commence his advance north towards Rabaul. The expansion of Dobodura to an airfield complex of a dozen runways paved the way for the capture of Lae, Salamaua and Finschhafen in September 1943 and United States Marine landings at Cape Gloucester, New Britain, in December.

The other way of looking at it is that at the end of the Papuan Campaign the front line was where it would have been had the Allies seized Buna in July, and established a garrison and airfield there, as they had intended to do in August, a month too late.

The Allied victories in Papua and Guadalcanal were intertwined. Support for the one necessarily was denial of support for the other. From September to December 1942, 310,000 tons of military cargo went from the US to the South Pacific Area, while only 157,000 tons went to MacArthur's South West Pacific Area. The 25th Infantry Division, slated for Australia, went

Low-level attacks on a Japanese convoy bound for Lae during the battle of the Bismarck Sea, March 1943. (Public domain via Wikimedia Commons)

to Guadalcanal instead. The emphasis on Guadalcanal was the Allied response to a decision made in Tokyo, that Guadalcanal was more important than Papua. The IJN agreed, its fleet carriers could operate freely east of the Solomon Islands in support of Guadalcanal, in the open ocean, but that was not the case in the relatively confined waters of the Solomon Sea off Papua with an increasingly powerful Allied air force at Port Moresby. Just as the Japanese denied Papua reinforcements, sending them to Guadalcanal, so the Americans found it necessary to maintain their forces at the latter, at the expense of the former.

9th Australian Division troops disembark at Red Beach, near Lae, September 1943. (Australian War Memorial 306542)

The outcome of the Papuan Campaign was not much influenced by air support on the battlefield: the Allies performed poorly at that and, for much of the campaign, IJN air was absent at Guadalcanal. Nor did the 5th Air Force's attempt to interdict the Japanese line of communication along the Sanananda road to the Kokoda Trail succeed – the September storms and rain reduced Japanese supply much more than aircraft could. What Allied airpower did achieve, by December 1942, was to deny the sea lane to Papua to transport ships. Thereafter only fast destroyers and submarines could deliver lesser amounts of cargo at night. There were no naval battles near Papua during the campaign. The naval battles that influenced it were fought in the Solomon Islands, near Guadalcanal.

About 22,000 Japanese fought on land in the Papuan Campaign. Some 3,500 left before the battle of Buna–Gona began – many of them construction troops – and 1,400 escaped from Milne Bay. Another 3,000 got away during the Buna breakout. The remaining 14,000 died. Allied propaganda accounts at the time recorded occasions when starving Japanese resorted to cannibalism. It did happen, at the *144th* roadblock at Buna for instance, but it was not widespread. Most Japanese still had at least a little food when their last positions in Papua were eliminated. The great majority of Japanese in Papua died in battle, not of starvation.

On land, 930 American servicemen died in Papua, another 310 in the air. Some 2,037 were wounded and 8,259 evacuated sick. The Australians had 2,134 dead, with 3,532 wounded. There were also 158 Papuans who died while serving with the Allies, and an unknown number died serving with the Japanese.

Some 16,000 American and 21,000 Australian soldiers fought in the campaign. Behind these combatants was an ever-growing logistics base, providing various kinds of support of which the Japanese could only dream. By November 1942, the Allies had 61,000 men in Papua, half of them in non-combat support roles in Port Moresby, Milne Bay and behind the fighting line at Buna.

# THE BATTLEFIELDS TODAY

## PORT MORESBY

Jackson Field (7 Mile Drome) was named in honour of Squadron Leader John Jackson, RAAF, killed in action in 1942. It is now Port Moresby International Airport, the normal point of entry to Papua New Guinea, the southern portion of which was, until 1975, the Territory of Papua. In Port Moresby, war relics can be seen at the National Museum. There are also fortifications, plane crash sites and shipwrecks relating to World War II. Ten miles out is Bomana Cemetery, where 3,824 Commonwealth servicemen are buried, including those from the Papuan Campaign. United States war dead from the campaign are buried in Manila or the United States.

Visiting the battlefields is rewarding, but not always easy or safe. They vary between untouched and those where villages have expanded across part of a battlefield. From Port Moresby there are flights to Milne Bay, Kokoda and Giruwa (for Buna–Gona). All these are easily visited, but the farther you go from the airport the more difficult it can be.

## KOKODA TRAIL

Japanese trenches at Ioribaiwa, 2022. (Author's Collection)

Over 80 years on, there is still no road over the Owen Stanley Range. There are helipads in a few villages, but otherwise to see the scenes of 1942, you must walk the Trail. It is as it was, a muddy, difficult trek. The Trail, starting outside Port Moresby at Ower's Corner, where Imita Ridge can be seen, to Kokoda, is 63 miles. It is a daunting task, but thousands walk it every year. It climbs over dozens of ridges, crossing as many deep gorges over fast-flowing rivers on tree trunk bridges. One mile an hour is good going. It can be done in five days if fit and keen, but a more leisurely pace of ten days enables one to linger over the scenes of fighting where trenches and rusted weapons can still be seen. Villages along the way display small collections of weapons and equipment. On the Isurava battlefield is the memorial to the Australians and Papuans who died.

As the Trail passes through tribal lands, where permission is needed to enter, it is not possible to walk it alone. However, there are many trekking companies that can organize a trip.

The north end of the Trail is Kokoda, where a good road goes to Sanananda, provided bridges and tarmac have not been washed away by storms or flood. Some of the Kokoda tour companies offer an extended trip to see the Buna–Sanananda–Gona battlefields.

## MILNE BAY

Milne Bay is easy to visit and it is safe to get around alone. A sealed road runs along the narrow flats on the north coast of the bay where the fighting took place. The town of Alotau now covers a portion of the area fought over. A drive from the bay the Japanese landed in to No 3 Strip, the furthest Japanese advance, is only 8 miles. Gurney airport, previously No 1 Strip, is 3 miles west of No 3 Strip. There is a monument to the battle, some World War II wreckage, basic signage at important locations, but no museum. Cruise ships often visit Milne Bay. They dock in the middle of the area that was fought over.

## BUNA–GONA

Like the Kokoda Trail, it would be best to arrange to visit with a tour company. The main town, Popondetta, is not safe for a lone tourist. Important sites such as Huggins roadblock are marked and Gona, Buna and Sanananda can all be reached by unsealed road from the airport. A walk along the beach from Buna to Sanananda, with the occasional creek crossing, is easily done, but to get to farther away spots such as Cape Endiadere, you need a guide to negotiate with the landowner. There is a wrecked World War II aircraft at Dobodura, where some runways can still be seen. There is a Stuart tank from the battle near Simemi Creek, a Japanese 3in gun and war museum at Buna and one or two places where bunkers can be seen, at the west end of Old Strip, for instance. However, the sandy soil by the sea, and time, has eroded most of the defences.

Dr Peter Williams and Squadron Leader Steven Daniels RAAF at the scene of Sergeant Bottcher's feat at Buna, where his platoon broke through. (Author's Collection)

The volcanic eruption of Mount Lamington in 1951 altered the wartime coastline somewhat. The swamps are not as extensive today as they were in 1942.

The Australian and United States governments sponsor searches for Australians and Americans still 'missing in action' in Papua. In Japan, private organizations, often regiment based, visit periodically to look for the thousands of Japanese still missing.

# FURTHER READING

Anderson, Nicholas, *The Battle of Milne Bay 1942*, Army History Unit: Canberra (2018)
Bullard, Steven (trans.), *Japanese Army Operations in the South Pacific Area: New Britain and Papua Campaigns 1942–43*, Australian War Memorial: Canberra (2007)
Dean, Peter, *MacArthur's Coalition: US and Australian Operations in the Southwest Pacific Area, 1942–1945*, University Press of Kansas: Lawrence, KS (2018)
James, Bill, *Field Guide to the Kokoda Track*, Kokoda Press: Lane Cove (2012)
Mayo, Lida, *Bloody Buna*, Australian National University Press: Canberra (1975)
McCarthy, Dudley, *South-West Pacific Area – First Year: Kokoda to Wau*, Australian War Memorial: Canberra (1959)
Milner, Samuel, *Victory in Papua: United States Army in World War II*, Center of Military History: Washington, DC (1989)
War Department, *Papuan Campaign: The Buna-Sanananda Operation, 16 November 1942-23 January 1943*, The Battery Press: Nashville, TN (1989)
Williams, Peter, *The Kokoda Campaign 1942: Myth and Reality*, Cambridge University Press: Cambridge (2012)

# INDEX

Figures in **bold** refer to illustrations.

Adachi Hatazo, Lieutenant General 72, 85
air support 6, 15, 17, **21**, 44–45, 57, 91
airfields 21
Allen, Major General Arthur **11**, 51, 52, 53, 54, 56
Allied Air Force 17, 51, 91
Allied forces
    air support 17, 44–45, 51, 57, 91
    artillery 88
    casualties 41, 86
    health 17
    infantry 16
    intelligence 22
    logistical support 17, 84
    orders of battle 18–19
    plan 22
    tanks 16–17
*Anshun* (Australian supply ship) 42
Australia 6–7, 7, 11, 12, 22
Australian Directorate of Naval Intelligence 22
Australian Imperial Force 6–7, **86**
    artillery 40, 51, **64**, 69, 70, 79
    casualties 25, 31, 35, 41, 42, 43, 44, 45, **48**, 49, 50, 51, 53, 54, 55–56, 63, 68, **78**, 82, 86, 89, 91
    divisions
        7th Division 12, **13**, 53, 56, 60–63
        9th Division **91**
    brigades
        16th Brigade 54, 55–56, 60, 64, 68–69, 83
        18th Brigade 75, **78**, 79, 86–87
        21st Brigade 49, 68, 82, 82–83
        25th Brigade 49, 53–56, 60, 61, 63–64
        30th Brigade 25, 82–83
    regiments
        6th Armoured Regiment 16–17, 75, **78**, 86, **86**
        7th Cavalry Regiment 83, 86
        126th Regiment 69, 71, 75, 79, 80
        144th Regiment **28**
    battalions
        3rd Battalion 61, 62, 63
        9th Battalion 41–42, **74**
        10th Battalion 39–40
        12th Battalion 41–42, 42, **85**
        14th Battalion 31, 35, 42–44, 44–45, **48**, 49
        16th Battalion 42–44, 44–45, **48**, 49, 68, 82
        27th Battalion 44–45, 49, 68, 82
        31st Battalion 50–51, 53, 61–62
        33rd Battalion 50–51, 53, 62
        39th Battalion 23, 25, 31, 35, 43, **43**, 82–83
        53rd Battalion 31, 34, 43
        61st Battalion 39, 40, 41
    health 17
    infantry 16
    logistical support 17, 52–53, **53**
    orders of battle 18–19
    tanks 16–17, 75, **78**, 79, 85
Australian New Guinea Administrative Unit 17, 31
Awala 23, **28**

Bismarck Sea, battle of the **90**
Blamey, General Thomas **11**, 12–13, 13, 22, 38, 53, 56, 57, 67, 72
Brigade Hill, battle of 10, 44–45, **48**, 49
Buna 7, 11, 13, 30, 38
Buna–Gona, battle of **13**, 14, 16, 17, 63–64, **64**, **65**, **66**, 88, **93**, 93
    Allied command 72
    American front 69–71, 85–86, **85**, **86**
    assessment 88–90
    Australian front 67–69, **68**, 82–84, **83**, 86–88
    casualties 12, 68, **70**, 87
    *coup de main* failure 71–72
    Japanese breakout 88
    Japanese command 72, 74
    Japanese defences 66, **66**, 75, **78**, 81
    orders of battle 19
    supply lines 84
    Urbana front 79–82, **79**, **80**, **81**, **82**
    Warren front 74–75, **74**, **75**, **78**, 79

Cameron, Major Allan 29–30
campaign
    aftermath 10, 90–91, **90**, **91**
    Allied thrust towards Buna 56–57, **58–59**, 60–63, **60**, **62**
    attack on Deniki 30
    battle of Brigade Hill 10, 44–45, **48**, 49
    battle of Efogi 10, 44, 49
    battle of Ioribaiwa 49–51
    battle of Isurava 30–31, **31**, **32–33**, 34–35
    battle of Milne Bay 16, 18, 36, **37**, **38–42**, **38**, **39**, **40**, **41**, 42
    battle of Oivi–Gorari 60–63, **60**, **62**
    first contact **28**
    First Eora–Templeton's 42–43
    Japanese advance on the Kokoda Trail 23, **23**, **24**, 25, **25**, **28**, 29–31, **29**, **31**, **32–33**, 34–35, **34**
    Japanese retreat 51–56
    Kokoda Trail 16, 17, 18, **43**
    landing at Basabua 23
    Second Eora–Templeton's 52–56
    Second Kokoda 29–30
Caro, Colonel Albert 44, 45
Carrier, Lieutenant Colonel Edmund 69, 75
casualties 30, 51, **88**, 91
    Brigade Hill 45, **48**
    Buna–Gona 12, 68, 70, 72, **78**, 80, 82, 86, **86**, 89
    disease 17
    Efogi 49
    First Eora–Templeton's 43, 44
    Ioribaiwa 50, 51
    Isurava 31, 35
    Japanese advance on the Kokoda Trail 25
    Milne Bay 41, 42
    Oivi–Gorari 63
    Second Eora–Templeton's 53, 54, 55–56
    Second Kokoda 30
Chalk, Lieutenant John 23, **28**
chronology 8–9
Citizen Military Force (CMF) 16
Clowes, Major General Cyril 22, **38**, 39–40, 41
Commonwealth Investigation Branch 22
Coral Sea, battle of the 6, 7, 22

Deniki 29, 30, 31
Dobbs, Lieutenant Colonel James 40
Dobodura 7, 22, 93
Duropa Plantation **74**, 75, **78**

Eather, Brigadier Ken 49–51, 51, 53, 61
Efogi, battle of 10, 44, 49
Eichelberger, Lieutenant General Robert 12, **12**, 72, 75
Eora Gorge 31, **31**, 34
Eora–Templeton's
    first action 42–44
    second action 52–56

Gama River 40, 41
Gona 67–68, 82–83
Grahamslaw, Captain Thomas **16**
Guadalcanal 6, 10, 15, 52, 55, 57, 72, 88, 90–91
Guam 10

Harding, Major General Edwin 12, **12**, 64, 72, 84
Herring, Lieutenant General Edmund 13, **13**, 53, 64, 67, 75, 86
Horie Masao, Major 34, 45
Horii Tomitaro, Major General 10, **11**, 31, 35, 49, 52, 53, 54, 54–55, 57, 60, 61, 62

Hyakutake Harukichi, Lieutenant General  6, 10, **10**, 21, 36, 52, 57, 72

Imamura Hitoshi, General  72, 88
Imperial Headquarters  6, 20
Imperial Japanese Army  14, 15, 61
    air support  15
    artillery  14, **14**, 23, **28**, 31, 35, 43, 50, 51, 54, 55, **62**, 63, **89**
    armies
        17th Army  6, 10, 62, 72
        18th Army  72
    brigades
        21st Mixed Brigade  11, 72, 74
    regiments
        15th Independent Engineer Regiment  23, 29–30, 49
        41st Regiment  14, 31, 35, 42–44, 52, 60–63, 67, 68, 82–83, **83**
        144th Regiment  5, 10, 14, 23, **25**, 29–30, 31, 34–35, 42, 44–45, **48**, 49, 50–51, 52, 53, 55–56, 60, 61–62, 62–63, 67, 68–69, 71, 83, 86–88, 91
        170th Regiment  14, 85–86
        229th Regiment  14, 69, 71
    battalions
        39th Battalion  29–30, 34
    casualties  30, 34, 35, 43, 44, 49, 51, 53, 54, 55–56, 63, 82, 86, **87**, 91
    health  15
    infantry  14
    intelligence  20, 56
    logistical support  15, **29**, 84
    *Nankai Shitai* (South Seas Force)  10, 14, 15, 20, 52, 62 plan 20–21
    orders of battle  18–19
    Stanley Detachment  52, 52–56
Imperial Japanese Navy  6, 20, 90, 91
    3rd Kure  40–41
    4th Fleet  6, 39
    5th Sasebo  38, 40–42, 71, 79, **82**
    8th Fleet Headquarters  38
    air support  15, 38
    casualties  41, 42
    Naval Pioneers  29–30, 39
    Special Naval Landing Force  14, 14–15, 38–42, 40, 42, 52, **56**, 57, 66
Ioribaiwa  10, 49–51, **92**
Isurava, battle of  10, 30–31, **31**, **32–33**, 34–35, 92

Katue, Sergeant Major  **16**
Kenney, General George  17, 51
Koiwai Mitsuo, Major  35, 43
Kokoda  22, **29**, **60**, 61, 63
    first battle of  25, 29, **29**
    second battle of  29–30

Kokoda Trail  10, 15, 16, 17, 18, 21, 22, **43**, 92–93
    Japanese advance  23, **23**, **24**, 25, **25**, **28**, 29–31, **29**, **31**, 32–33, 34–35, **34**
Kumusi River  **23**, 25, 57, 61
Kusunose Masao, Colonel  10, **11**, 45, 49, 49–50, 52, 63

Lae  7, 10, 22, 90, **91**
Lloyd, Brigadier John  54, 55

MacArthur, General Douglas  7, 11–12, **11**, 12, 13, 22, 38, 52, 53, 56, 57, 72, 86, 90
McCoy, Lieutenant Colonel Robert  69, 70
*Manunda* (Australian hospital ship)  42
Martin, Colonel Clarence  74–75
Midway, battle of  6, 7
Mikawa Gunichi, Admiral  36, 42
Miller, Lieutenant Colonel Kelsie  69, 70
Milne Bay  7, 14–15, 22, 52, 56, 57, 93
    airstrips  36, 39, 39, 40–41, 41, 93
    battle of  18, 36, 37, 38–42, 38, 39, 40, 41
    strategic importance  21, 38

New Guinea  6, 7
New Guinea Administrative Unit  25
New Guinea Force  12, 13
Nishimura Kokichi, Corporal  **48**

Ogawa Tetsuo, Captain  23, **28**, 29
Oivi–Gorari  **13**, 14, 25, 60–63, **60**, **62**
orders of battle  18–19
Orokaiva  25, 29–30
Owen, Colonel William  25, 29
Owen Stanley Range  7, 20, 21, **29**, 55, 66

Papua  6, 10, 11, 20–21, 22
Papuan Infantry Battalion  16, **16**, 22, 25, **28**, 30, 31, 44
Port Moresby  6, 7, 13, 16, 20, 21, **21**, 22, 29, 30, 49, 52, 56, 91, 92
Porter, Brigadier Selwyn  49–51, 83
Potts, Brigadier Arnold  31, 34, 35, 44, 45, 49
prisoners of war  89, **89**

Rabaul  5, 6, 10, 17, 22
Rowell, Major General Sydney  12, 13, 35, 40, 44, 53
Royal Australian Air Force  17, 38, 39, 51, 80
Royal Papuan Constabulary  25, 31, 44

Salamaua  7, 10, 22, 90
Samari Island  21, 36
Sanananda  68–69, 82, 83–84, **83**
Simemi Creek  69, 74–75, 79, **79**, **82**, 93
Solomon Islands  6, 15
strategic situation, 1942  5–7

Takeda Tsuneyoshi, Prince  20
tanks  16–17, 39, **40**, 75, **78**, 79, 85, 88
Tol Plantation massacre  10
Tomlinson, Colonel Clarence  69, 79, 80
Tsukamoto Hatsuo, Lieutenant Colonel  10, 29–30, 54, 55, 87

United States Army Air Force (USAAF)  16, 17
US Army  64
    artillery  17, 64, **81**
    casualties  12, 42, 70, 72, 80, 86, 89, 91
    corps
        1st Corps  7, 12
    divisions
        25th Infantry Division  90–91
        32nd Infantry Division  12, 16, 17, 52, 57, 64, 64, 66, 72, 79, 79–80, 84
        41st Division  12, 16, 72
    regimental combat teams
        126th Regimental Combat Team  63, 69–70, 89
        127th Regimental Combat Team  74, 79–80, **79**, 82, 85
        128th Regimental Combat Team  63, 69–70, 71, 75, **78**, 79, 80
        163rd Regimental Combat Team  16, 86–88
    infantry  16, **75**
    logistical support  17
    orders of battle  18–19
    Urbana Force  71, 79–82, **79**, **80**, **81**, **82**
    Warren Force  69–70, 74–75, **74**, **75**, **78**, 79
US Navy  5–6, 36, 57

Vasey, Major General George  13, **13**, 60, 61, 63, 64, 66, 68, 83–84, 86–87

Watson, Major William  23, **28**

Yamagata Tsuyuo, Lieutenant General  11, 74, 88
Yamamoto Tsunichi, Major  82, 85
Yano Minoru, Commander  40–41, 41
Yazawa Kiyomi, Colonel  43, 44, 49
Yokoyama Yosuke, Colonel  20, 23